SYNAST

A comprehensive guide to the art o[illegible] comparison, including detailed interpretations of the Elements, Qualities, planets, angles and inter-aspects in synastric analysis and in-depth case studies.

By the same author:

ROMANCING THE STARS

Also in this series:

ASTROLOGER'S COMPANION John & Peter Filbey

ASTROLOGICAL COUNSELLING Christina Rose

ASTROLOGY OF KARMA Pauline Stone

ASTRONOMY FOR ASTROLOGERS John & Peter Filbey

BOOK OF WORLD HOROSCOPES Nicholas Campion

CHART SYNTHESIS Roy Alexander

CHINESE ASTROLOGY Derek Walters

DARK STARS Bernard Fitzwalter & Raymond Henry

DRACONIC ASTROLOGY Pamela A.F. Crane

FORECASTING BY ASTROLOGY Martin Freeman

HARMONIC CHARTS David Hamblin

HORARY ASTROLOGY Derek Appleby

HOW TO INTERPRET A BIRTH CHART Martin Freeman

HOW TO RECTIFY A BIRTH CHART Laurie Efrein

JUNGIAN BIRTH CHARTS Arthur Dione

MUNDANE ASTROLOGY Michael Baigent, Nicholas Campion & Charles Harvey

NATAL CHARTING John Filbey

SOLAR AND LUNAR RETURNS John Filbey

TWELVE HOUSES Howard Sasportas

SYNASTRY

A Comprehensive Guide to the Astrology of Relationships

by

Penny Thornton, D.F.Astrol.S.

Text illustrations by the author

THE AQUARIAN PRESS

First published 1982

British Library Cataloguing in Publication Data

Thornton, Penny
Synastry: a comprehensive guide to
the astrology of relationships
1. Astrology
I. Title
133.5 BF1708

ISBN 0-85030-276-5

The Aquarian Press is part of the Thorsons Publishing Group, Wellingborough, Northamptonshire, NN8 2RQ, England

Printed in Great Britain by
Woolnough Bookbinding Limited, Irthlingborough, Northamptonshire

5 7 9 11 13 15 14 12 10 8 6

CONTENTS

TO MY PARENTS

for their loving support and encouragement

ACKNOWLEDGEMENTS

Writing itself may be a solitary toil, but producing a book demands a team of efficient, co-operative, patient workers. I am therefore indebted to Marjorie Horsfield for her long hours of typing, Chester Kemp for his critique and my publishers, The Aquarian Press. But most of all my deepest appreciation and thanks to my husband, Simon, without whose 'red pen', this manuscript would have been incomprehensible! Indeed a labour of love.

INTRODUCTION

Even the rainbow has a body
made of drizzling rain
and it is an architecture of glistening atoms
built up, built up
yet you can't lay your hand on it,
nay not even your mind.

D. H. Lawrence,
The Rainbow

Most people when embarking on the study of astrology do so for a variety of reasons, but in the main, it is the element of mystery, the seeking of hidden knowledge that fascinates. Once the initial spark is lit and the search begun, then Pandora's box is well and truly open. How often, though, the early enthusiasm wanes as the more dreary aspects of calculation and interpretation emerge; but to the real astrologer no obstacle is too great: the quest for knowledge, truth and meaning draws him ever deeper, opening up vast levels of experience and revealing an increasingly subtle and splendid inner language.

All astrologers fall into the trap of Sun sign generalities at some point in their work; indeed, parts of this book deal with broad zodiacal categories and the interaction between them. Yet it cannot be emphasized too often, that the Sun sign is virtually only one-tenth of the whole picture and the complex structure of planets, signs and houses is where the real understanding of the true nature of astrology begins. So often one encounters hard scientific argument against the validity of astrology based purely on Sun sign observations. Yet one only has to grasp some fundamental aspects of astrology to appreciate its real beauty as a system.

Certainly astrology has been with us a long time, although its earliest origins are lost in the ancient mystery schools.[1] One can assume, however, that as soon as man was able to relate the seasons

[1] Star charts from Ancient Egypt reliably dated from around 4200 B.C. have survived, although the Chaldeans are usually recognized as the earliest exponents of horoscopic astrology, as we know it today.

to the presence of particular constellations and observe the changing face of the Moon, that the study of the stars had begun.

For the past two millenia, astrology encountered periods of acceptance from astronomers, philosophers and scientists, but by the dawning of the Age of Reason in the eighteenth century it had begun its sad decline. Only at the turn of this century, with the work of such astrologers as Alan Leo and Charles Carter and the esoteric doctrines of Alice Bailey and Madame Blavatsky, did astrology begin to re-emerge. As recently as the 1960s astrology experienced a popular renaissance and, in a way, it is from those 'flower-power' seeds that today's astrology is burgeoning forth. Instead of the earlier accent on prognostication, the focus has shifted to counselling and the development of insight and self-awareness, making astrology a sensitive psychological tool. In fact, the very word psychology is taken from the two Greek words, psyche (soul) and logos (wisdom) and soul-searching has always been the province of astrology.

However, it should not be forgotten that modern-day astrologers owe a good deal to the ancient exponents of their craft whose degree of intuitive thought gave them considerable accuracy in prognostication and much wisdom in comprehending man's consciousness. In fact all the energy and interest that Western man now devotes to science and technology were once applied to the esoteric and the intuitive.

Astrology is both a science and an art, and although practitioners tend to fall into one camp or another, both are essential to each other. Without the ability to stand back and question its principles, astrology would amount to vague, mystic ramblings and may never have left the pier or the magazine columns. Yet, in order to bring meaning out of the symbols and to impart the information to someone else, one needs to be an artist.

This would be an apt point at which to unveil how astrology works but unfortunately this is not possible. It appears that thus far we are trying to explain the unknowable and measure the immeasurable and until perhaps we can find the right approach by which to assess the system in purely scientific terms, we shall have to be content with the fact that it is largely a belief-system.[2] It may

[2] Present day research into astrology using statistical analysis and computerized data is producing a more empirical base for astrology, e.g. Michel Gauquelin's excellent work with the prominence of certain planets in the diurnal (daily) circle. But as Ralph Metzner points out in his book *Maps of Consciousness*, 'data has to be somehow integrated into framework of the current scientific paradigm . . .'.

be that as we begin to comprehend more about our perception of reality the complex interaction between man and the cosmos will be understood. Until then the axiom 'As above, so below' is a good foundation upon which to place one's beliefs. In working with astrology the pattern of the planets at birth can be seen to mirror the individual's psyche, and in time, the planets' movements reflect the individual's development.

If one adopts a more spiritual stance, it could be said that the chart is chosen by the incarnating soul in order to experience specific earth lessons, and so the concept of karma (the spiritual law of cause and effect) is implicit in astrology.

Astrologers frequently refer to the horoscope as a map, which is a good way of allowing the individual to see his life as a kind of journey. The route is portrayed by the planets, signs and houses, but the journey itself is unique. The more self-aware the individual becomes, the more his experience is enriched.

> Experience is not so much what
> happened to you, but what you did
> with what happened to you.
>
> *(Voltaire)*

In looking at astrology in the way of growth and awareness, Alice Bailey, in her book *Esoteric Astrology*, maintained that there are two different kinds of astrology: that of 'Man on the wheel' and that of 'Man on the path'. 'Man on the wheel', who is not consciously searching for a purpose, is completely conditioned and controlled by the planets, but the moment he becomes aware of his soul 'and is endeavouring to control his own path in life, the influence of the planets per se, definitely weakens'.

This way of looking at astrology appears to allow the individual an element of choice as to how his life will ultimately unfold, albeit through recognizing his own inner potential (or perhaps his soul's purpose) and it underlines the fundamental difference in philosophy between Eastern and Western astrologers. The idea of fate being all-powerful is inherent in Hindu astrology. This parallels the sharp inequality of Indian life, where the acceptance of one's circumstances is the only possible attitude where change seems impossible. In the West, by contrast, man seeks to better himself, regarding his circumstances as being alterable by his own intervention.

However, cosy as it may be to assume the free will aspect of astrology in the West, one only has to work in astrological practice for a few years to see how often fate seems to take a hand, and no other area of astrology seems so infused with 'destiny' as that of relationships.

From the moment we are born we begin to relate, firstly to our parents and closest relatives, then to our friends and other people outside the family circle; but the relationships that cause us the greatest extremes of happiness and despair are those in which we experience our deepest emotional and sexual response, and in the main this is encountered in marriage. For this reason I have decided to concentrate on these types of relationships in this book.

'No man is an island' is a cliché that like all clichés contains an element of truth; no matter how self-contained an individual may be, he has to relate to the outside world in some way even if he ultimately rejects it to enter a monastery, and even then he is bound to relate to his fellow monks. The only way we discover truths about ourselves is through the reaction of others, and although loving parents may be blind to the faults of an adored child, companions, colleagues and peers tend not to wear the same rose-coloured spectacles. The interplay of human relationships is the most important factor in guiding us to a degree of self-awareness, and as with many things in life, the most difficult and testing experiences give us the most insight and thereby produce the most growth.

In some ways, the art of achieving successful relationships can appear to be a sort of 'chicken and egg' situation. One needs to relate in order to find out who one is, yet until one really knows who one is, relationships, in the main, can be highly unsatisfactory. Certainly we get the relationships we deserve, whether we take this to mean that like attracts like or adopt the karmic idea of destined meetings and relationships. Whatever the reason, the astrological detail is often the most illuminating factor of all in describing the type of relationships likely to be encountered and the interplay of the relationships themselves. An individual who expresses the central theme of rejection and disappointment in his chart, naturally gets rejected and disappointed, and until there is a shift in attitude and awareness, matters are unlikely to improve.

It is often when trying to solve a relationship dilemma that the individual seeks an answer in astrology, for no system seems to be able to give such a fine perspective on a situation. The horoscope is not only an excellent psycho-spiritual map, a guide to inner workings, but has the added dimension of being an accurate time chart. With the advent of psycho-analysis, encounter groups and awareness programmes of all sorts, astrology is beginning to find its role increasingly in the area of counselling. Not all astrologers are counsellors of course, but in going through the intricacies of a horoscope in person-to-person consultation, advice is inevitably sought, particularly at major turning-points in the life, and nine times out of ten, these turning points involve relationships. Therefore, the understanding of human relationships through astrology-synastry (derived from the Greek prefix *syn*, meaning a bringing together, and *astron*, star) is one of the most important and specialized aspects of astrology as a whole.

During the course of my work as a consultant astrologer I ask for birth details not only of clients themselves, but of partners and families as well (providing, of course, I have permission). This has provided me both with a considerable amount of charts and a vast reservoir of information regarding synastry between people. In the following chapters most of the traditional methods of chart comparison will be covered as well as some of the newer ones; but as with any technique, it is a bare scaffolding which requires experience to produce the building.

There are of course, many pitfalls for the astrologer in assessing compatibility between two individuals. Even though the lines of communication as seen through the inter-aspects can appear inordinately difficult at times, one can by no means assume the relationship will end in outright disaster. If two people have enough love for each other and really *want* to make the relationship work, work it will in spite of the difficulties. If the couple are aware of their own and each other's psychological weaknesses and strengths, then potentially difficult 'energies' can be understood and overcome. In some cases, instead of representing severe psychological blocks that eventually undermine the relationship, the difficult aspects actually represent challenging external circumstances that unite a couple rather than alienate them. In a sense the difficulties become stepping stones to greater understanding. In the main, however, a plethora of difficult aspects and divergent astrological 'energies' will indicate a problematic relationship.

In my own experience, couples planning to marry usually approach an astrologer hoping to reinforce their ideas and their feelings, not to listen to conflicting ones, and if problems are pointed out to them, they will go ahead regardless. Fortunately, synastry can be used at *any* stage of a relationship to shed light on the situation, not merely at the beginning. As an astrologer, one can only give guidance; one cannot change the divine plan or people's minds. Perhaps this is why the old custom in India of arranged marriages based on astrological compatibility seems somehow morally and spiritually wrong. Ideally, one should have the freedom to make a choice, backed up with astrological insight. Perhaps in the future, engaged couples will make two important visits before their wedding-day: one to the minister and one to the astrologer!

Despite the alarming rise in the divorce rate and the increase of couples living together, marriage, apparently, has never been so popular. Yet why with all the advantages of our sophisticated and streamlined society are happiness and harmony such elusive qualities? The answer may be that man by nature needs a degree of friction in order to survive — a pattern which one can observe only too well on both a global level and in the domestic sphere. However, there is a spiritual philosophy that suggests man is evolving towards a more enlightened world, and in order to bring this about he must first create harmony within himself.

So far I have endeavoured to put forward astrology in as comprehensive a manner as possible, touching only fleetingly on its more spiritual connotations. However, the more one works with astrology in practice, the more one is aware of the spiritual dimension behind many of life's experiences. Over the past two or three years I have noticed an increase in the number of couples who feel they have been drawn together for a reason and who have an extraordinary level of attunement to each other. In some cases this has involved total upheaval and trauma, in divorcing previous partners or leaving jobs, families and even countries. The interesting thing is that it has been happening right through the age spectrum, from twenty-year-olds who have comparatively little experience to draw on, to seventy-year-olds with thirty-five years of marriage behind them. This could be purely coincidental, but in discussing my views with other astrologers, counsellors and spiritual advisers, I have found that I am not alone in my feelings. According to some spiritual and esoteric teachings, we are approaching a period of great change[3] and on a spiritual level a new order is emerging. In preparation for these changes, twin-souls are being allowed to meet. Perhaps to some, this amounts to nothing more than romantic fantasy, but to couples whose sense of destiny is exceedingly strong, there is recognition of a profound truth here.

Love has been the source of inspiration for thousands of years —

[3]Various cultures and religions contain the idea of huge cycles of time (world ages), the present one of which is drawing to a close. Astrologically speaking, we are moving from the Age of Pisces to the Age of Aquarius.

wars have been fought for love, cities and monuments built for love, epic poems and stories written about it. The experience of love is said to be an aspect of the divine working through man. The purpose of this book, however, is not to seek out the divine aspect of relationships, but to outline the ways astrology symbolizes the dialogue between people. The limitation of the book, and indeed of teaching any interpretive astrological technique, is in putting across the essential ingredient — intuition — which one needs to develop in order to assess the real essence between a couple. One cannot see the divine thread or for that matter the chemistry itself in astrological symbolism, merely the dialogue. Yet in comprehending the dialogue one has a valuable key to understanding why some relationships prove difficult and others easy. In becoming conscious of the differences between people and allowing for them, one becomes not only more tolerant, but increasingly aware, which goes a long way to creating harmony within oneself and with others.

1.
THE ELEMENTS AND QUALITIES

Earthly joy is rules and impediment;
aquatic joy is softness and repose
fiery pleasure is desire and love;
airy delight is liberty and movement.

Gaston Bachelard

In teaching astrology in the classroom, it became apparent that after going through the technicalities of calculation and the meanings of the planets and the signs, by the time information on the houses and aspects was introduced, the student was fighting his way through an ever thickening wood. To bring some order out of the chaos and enable the student to find any sense at all in what he was faced with, a focus was needed. The most immediate feature of a natal chart apart from rising planets is the particular emphasis in elements and signs (see Figure 2). For instance, a person who is born with four planets in Cancer, two in Pisces, two in Virgo, one in Gemini and one in Taurus has a water emphasis; so basically he is a responsive, instinctive, impressionable individual whose emotional well-being is of primary importance to the success of his life. This can be established before any in-depth analysis of the whole chart.

The four elements, fire, earth, air and water are central to the study of astrology. Indeed most metaphysical and psychological systems have a four-fold division contained within them. In the Middle Ages men were divided into four temperaments, choleric (fire), melancholic (earth), sanguine (air), and phlegmatic (water). Behaviour, illness and many other aspects of man's being were attributed to these four ideas. In modern physics the four states of matter are solid (earth), liquid (water), gaseous (air) and plasma or radiant ionized energy (fire). In fact the adjectives themselves, fiery, watery, earthy and airy-fairy are commonplace in our vocabulary and still retain their original meaning.

One of the most important links astrology has made with psychology is the association of the four elements with Jung's four psychological types, intuitive (fire), thinking (air), sensation (earth)

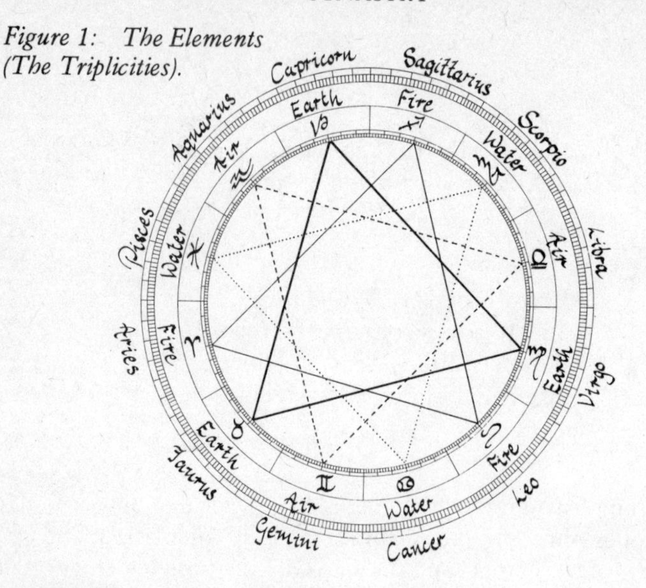

Figure 1: The Elements (The Triplicities).

and feeling (water).[1] In *Astrology, Psychology and the Four Elements*, Stephen Arroyo puts forward the idea of elements being forms of energy and stresses their importance in astrology: 'The interpretation of astrological charts takes on a new and deeper meaning when emphasis is put on the elements; for in this way one is dealing with specific life energies at work . . .'.

If we refer to the example of the individual with four planets in Cancer and two in Pisces, not only is there a preponderance of water, but a complete lack of planets in one element — fire. When an imbalance like this occurs, unless the individual is an astrologer or undergoing analysis, he is unlikely to be conscious of a missing function, in this case fire; but when he tries to express the exuberance or initiative associated with this element he finds enormous difficulty in doing so. Consequently, the individual will gravitate to people who 'radiate' this element, or project the necessary qualities on to them. One of the most noticeable facets of synastry is the individual's attraction for people who exemplify what he himself lacks. Yet because it is largely unconscious and foreign to his own more familiar traits, eventually that which attracts, repels.

To illustrate this example a little more: if the predominantly water type is involved in a relationship with a fiery individual, he

[1] For a real understanding of this concept, one should read *Relating* by Liz Greene.

Figure 2:

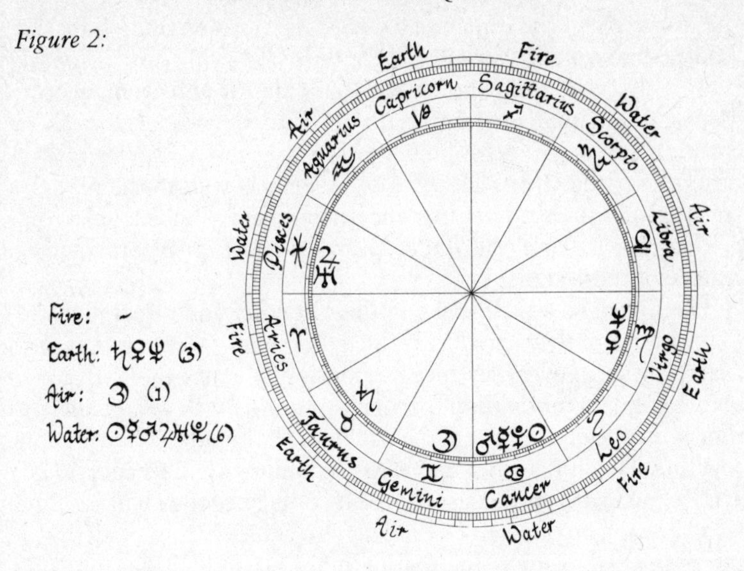

will initially be attracted by the inexhaustible supply of energy and charisma of fire and its extrovert, spontaneous nature; but after a while, the water individual will sense that he is never truly at peace in fire's presence and is continually trampled on and misunderstood. By contrast, the fire individual who was initially drawn to water's mystery, sensitivity and gentleness, will be irritated by the inconsistent moods and emotional demands of the water type.

Seeing the elements as life energies at work is particularly fascinating in synastry, for the idea of people's energy-fields interacting is a very visual and easy-to-understand mechanism for the attract-repel syndrome in relationships. The descriptions that follow, although generalized, outline the characteristics of the fire, earth, air and water signs. The understanding of the temperamental differences inherent in the elements, and the interchange of those energies between two individuals, is the most basic but informative feature of synastry.

The Element FIRE (Aries, Sagittarius and Leo)

The alchemists conceptualized fire as 'an element which operates in the centre of things' and a shared feature of the fire signs is the desire to be in the centre of activity and a tendency to be self-centred. Think of fire, and colour, warmth and energy spring to mind; all the qualities synonymous with fire signs. In fact the Sun itself is the ruler of one fire sign (Leo) and exalted in another (Aries). Sagittarius, Leo and Aries share a vitality and enthusiasm for life that make them the unparalleled optimists and adventurers of the Zodiac. In myth, fire was thought to be sacred to the gods because it represented spiritual knowledge, difficult though it may be to associate spiritual qualities with the fire signs as they charge through life apparently indifferent to the needs and feelings of others. Yet the strong idealism of fire adapts well to the idea of a spiritual quest or adventure and their courage and loyalty to a person (particularly the underdog) or a cause is an outstanding feature of these signs.

The fire signs are childlike in their honesty and directness and, like children, they give very little thought to the reality and practicalities of everyday life. Responsibility is not their strongest suit, but given motivation (particularly in the way of a challenge) they will accomplish more in a day than all the other elements put together. Nothing is impossible to predominantly fiery individuals and imbued with enthusiasm and self-confidence they will cut their way through any amount of red tape to achieve their objective. If the going gets rough, they will simply blast their way out of a situation. One of the drawbacks of too much fire, however, is the tendency to be overpowering and insensitive and to leave jobs half-finished when the novelty has worn off.

Fire in a chart represents the creative potential that puts ideas into action and encourages others to do the same. With a lack of this element, the individual may hide his light under a bushel and admire or resent others' ability to achieve what he can only do in his day-dreams. Individuals with plenty of fire in their charts (particularly involving the personal planets) take the initiative not only in achieving their goals but in forming relationships and directing them. Their needs and desires are plainly obvious. Fire is warm and affectionate and needs a good response to keep it burning.

The Element EARTH (Taurus, Virgo and Capricorn)

Gravity compels all objects to Earth, where in the main the ground is solid, sure and largely immovable. Earth represents the physical and the tangible and Capricorn, Taurus and Virgo are signs that are in touch with the physical senses and concerned with practical issues. In contrast to fire, which acts on impulse and intuition, the earth signs are premeditative and cautious, placing their faith in that which is visible, reliable and ultimately useful.

As the earth element falls into 'negative'[2] or introverted signs,

[2] The use of 'negative' in this context applies astrologically to the even numbered signs of the Zodiac and not to the dictionary definition of the word.

Capricorn, Virgo and Taurus are reluctant to thrust themselves into the limelight; however, if invited they perform very well. The earth signs have good organizing ability and put stability and endurability into situations. Unlike fire, earth is better at establishing that which has already been created and enjoys reward for effort in more tangible terms than merely the thrill of the challenge. In as much as fire makes good beginnings and tails off when the initial enthusiasm wanes, earth doggedly persists at his labours and frequently clears up after fire. When accused of behaving in a narrow-minded or pessimistic way, the earth signs often insist they are merely being realistic.

With feet firmly planted in the physical and material world, it may be enormously difficult to get the earth signs to place any value whatsoever on the ephemeral or the intangible. Yet beneath their conservative and practical bent is a yearning to experience the transcendental. As they are exceedingly physical types they often put up with relationships that are not only difficult but provide no emotional satisfaction; in fact, however, like the need for transcendence in the spiritual sense, the earthy type often craves an all-consuming passion.

Earth in a chart represents the structural and the tangible. It brings possibilities in to actuality and sees things through to the end. People with earth predominating in a chart can be painstaking and dependable and tend to treat life as a serious business. If a lack of earth is shown in a chart, then the individual is likely to be out of touch with the practical facts of life. This causes him to hold those who epitomize order and reliability in awe or contempt.

The Element AIR (Gemini, Libra and Aquarius)

The element air is synonymous with the realm of ideas and the intellect which is a human function. Indeed most of the signs of the Zodiac have animal symbolism with the exception of the air signs, two of which are represented in human form.[3] Like fire, the element air falls in 'positive' and extrovert signs and consequently these two are highly compatible. They are both outgoing and free-thinking in essence, and fire can be said to warm air by enthusing and inspiring its intellectual capabilities, whereas air usually fans the flames of fire, creating more action and desire.

Gemini, Aquarius and Libra are sociable and people-orientated

[3] Virgo is represented by a human symbol (Woman) and it is interesting to observe that this earth sign is notable for its intellectual capabilities and mental orientation.

signs and their informed conversation and friendly approach make them popular. They are logical, rational and objective and prefer to conceptualize than rush into action (like fire) or adhere to routine and cautious opinion (like earth).

If there is a problem with the air signs, then it is the difficulty they experience in finding their feelings and relating to people on an emotional level. The air signs, particularly Gemini, are better at writing about their feelings or analyzing them. Libra, although a sign embodying the principle of relating, still remains primarily concerned with the intellectual balance of relationships and the fair and just action of those participating. Aquarius personifies the idea of brotherhood and humanity as a whole and has more trouble in relating on a one-to-one emotional basis than Gemini and Libra put together.

The ability to debate, to bring clear-thinking objectivity to situations is the forte of the air signs. Without the intellectual vision and impartial judgement of air, the headstrong action of fire and the material pursuits of earth, would lack perspective.

Air in a chart represents the ability to conceptualize, to communicate and to appreciate cultural values. An individual with a preponderance of planets in air, whilst exemplifying these civilized aspects of man's nature, may fall short in his sensitivity to others. If there is a lack of air in a chart the individual may be unable to rationalize his actions and those of others or absorb intellectual ideas and communicate his own. Thus he may put intellectual types on a pedestal or criticize them for lack of feeling.

The Element WATER (Cancer, Scorpio and Pisces)

Water can be seen as the most essential element to all life; it circulates throughout the whole of nature in the form of rain, sap, milk and blood and in India it is regarded as the preserver of life itself. In fact the water signs (Cancer, Scorpio and Pisces) are considered to be extremely fertile. Water, like earth, is found in negative, introverted signs and these two elements are sympathetic to each other. If fire is associated with action and energy, earth with stability and structure, air with ideas and communication, then water is synonymous with feeling and subtlety. Cancer, Scorpio and Pisces are 'feminine'[4] signs ruled respectively by the Moon, Pluto and Neptune and these signs embody psychic sensitivity,

[4]Feminine here refers to the signs Taurus, Cancer, Virgo, Scorpio, Capricorn and Pisces. Like the word 'negative', it does not mean what the dictionary definition implies.

compassion and understanding. The ability of water to fill any container, pouring into the smallest gullies and cracks, its dark depths and unpredictable behaviour are all symbolic of water's nature. Water types are tuned to the subliminal and the unconscious and react to the emotional impact of a situation and the subtle undercurrents of life.

The water signs are sometimes looked upon as the woolly-minded and less intellectually perspicacious members of the Zodiac (particularly Pisces) yet these signs have enormous stores of wisdom and understanding. What they lack is the self-confidence of fire or the rational flexibility of air to impart their ideas or explain the mechanics of them. Artists and mystics frequently have water signs emphasized in their charts as they bring aspects of the transcendental into man's experience.

As the water element occurs in signs at the end of each four-fold series (Aries-fire; Taurus-earth; Gemini-air; Cancer-water, etc.) they can be seen as both the fulfilment of one cycle and the beginning of another. It is as though water brings together all dimensions of experience and synthesizes them in order to bring about new growth.

Water can be the most inscrutable and secretive element of the Zodiac. Cancer, Scorpio and Pisces have all sorts of defences to prevent people from seeing their vulnerability, yet in many ways they are the most easily hurt and manipulated of the signs.

Water in a chart represents emotional depth and instinctive understanding. An individual with too much water in a chart, however, may be rather subjective and too absorbed in his feelings to grasp the reality of a situation, whereas an individual with a lack of this element may be unable to feel sympathy or compassion for others and may have difficulty in expressing his own feelings. Thus he may well admire or resent those who radiate sensitivity and who regard the material things of life as being secondary to inner values.

Having established the element bias in the horoscope, the placing of the signs in their respective *quadruplicities*, cardinal, fixed and mutable, is another good indicator of basic temperament and inclination. Each element in its triplicity is represented by a different quality and as the qualities fall in signs that are 90° and 180° apart (or in square and opposition to one another), they form the grand-crosses of astrology.

The CARDINAL Signs (Aries, Cancer, Libra and Capricorn)
The textbook keyword for CARDINAL, is action, and Aries,

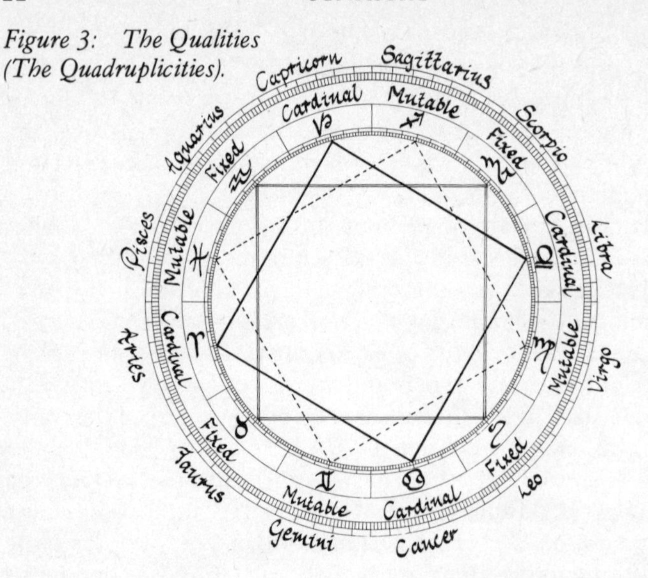

Figure 3: The Qualities (The Quadruplicities).

Capricorn, Cancer and Libra share the desire to achieve and the ability to initiate action on their own behalf. Although the desires for action and achievement may differ, the underlying theme remains constant: the urge to succeed, to gain prominence and to accept challenge.

The idea of challenge may not initially sound like a Cancerian quality, but many student astrologers mistakenly assume that Cancer, because it is a water sign, is passive and therefore non-achieving. This, of course, is where the idea of cardinality becomes complicated because its action, and initiation keywords have to filter through a sensitive, feeling water sign. Cancer may not actively seek out challenge, but if it sees something it wants it will persistently move towards its objective, spending huge amounts of emotional energy in circumnavigation and defence mechanisms.

Cardinality seems best suited to fire so that Aries as the only cardinal fire sign is about as pure unadulterated fire as one could hope to find. Aries, the pioneer, is first off the mark to launch itself impulsively into experience, particularly in pursuit of its own ambitions. Aries feels no one can do anything as well or as quickly as he does. Combined with its strong will, Aries often alienates people and thus becomes labelled (mistakenly) as a loner. In contrast, Libra, its opposite sign, seeks harmony and perfection in relationships and the pursuit of joint goals. Libra is cardinal and air, so although the action and ambition of this sign is not seen in such physically active terms as Aries, it none the less enjoys the challenge of debate and discussion. Libra is adept at initiating social intercourse, which can sometimes appear to onlookers as downright social-climbing. The cardinal action of Capricorn can be seen, rather like Cancer, in the dogged pursuit of its aims. The effect of cardinality in an earth element is reminiscent of a large boulder making its way down a gradual incline, gathering momentum towards the end of its journey, and arriving with great impact. Capricorn, more than the other cardinal signs, relishes the glory of being at the top.

A predominantly cardinal person is enterprising, self-motivated and ambitious, and those who lack this quality may resist opportunity and lack the desire or ability to get their ideas off the ground.

The FIXED Signs (Leo, Taurus, Scorpio and Aquarius)

Our normal use of the word FIXED is eminently descriptive of this astrological quality. Taurus, Leo, Scorpio and Aquarius seek to establish that which cannot be altered or moved. There is a common rigidity and inflexibility with these signs and an inbuilt dislike of change. Their natural reserve guards them against rushing into action and they often appear to block the actions of others.

Although these qualities may be easily observable with Taurus, Scorpio and Leo, Aquarius, because it is an air sign, appears to be the odd man out. Rational Aquarius, apparently open to alternative possibilities, will remain stubbornly attached to his own opinions and with eloquent and articulate speech convince his opponents that black is really white. Aquarius is also consistent in his unpredictable behaviour.

Taurus epitomizes the concept of fixity. As fixed earth, Taurus remains rooted to his physical senses and seeks material and financial security. Although essentially a placid sign, the threat of losing his possessions or accepting change can galvanize him into fairly aggressive action. Scorpio, the opposite sign is fixed water, and as water is a feeling element this sign seeks stability and permanence in relationships and emotional security. The reluctance of Scorpio to let go emotionally and his proneness to paranoia, lead this sign into emotional trauma and crisis all too often. Leo, as fixed fire, is at best tremendously powerful and self-expressive, and at worst bombastic and egotistical. This sign loves power, luxury and wealth and gravitates to positions of authority.

An individual with a preponderance of planets in fixed signs is likely to be persistent and purposeful, yet resistant to change and somewhat opinionated and fanatical. An individual lacking fixity in his chart may be unstable and purposeless.

The MUTABLE Signs (Gemini, Virgo, Sagittarius and Pisces)

MUTABLE signs are said to be adaptable and dispersive. In other words, Gemini, Virgo, Sagittarius and Pisces tend to scatter their interests rather than express the dynamism of the cardinal signs or the firmness of purpose of the fixed. The mutable signs also seek to acquire knowledge and disseminate it. In this quadruplicity Virgo seems out of place where the scattering of interests is concerned, as this sign has a penchant for detail and concentrated effort. Yet Virgo is a many-talented sign and its innate sense of service brings it into contact with a variety of people and a wide experience.

Air is most easily identifiable with mutability in its mental orientation and flexibility. Gemini, as mutable air, is versatile in mind and limb but its restless, enquiring nature and multi-faceted personality can also lack depth and staying-power. Sagittarius is mutable fire, and the spirit of adventure of this fire sign is reflected in its liking for distant horizons and religious and philosophical pursuits. Sagittarius is sometimes accused of having 'its head in the clouds', preferring intellectual interests to mundane matters. Pisces, as mutable water, is possibly the most elusive to grasp of all the mutuable signs. Here the boundaries of experience both inner and outer are limitless, making Pisces a virtual puppet of the unconscious and subject to its own changeable feelings and those of others.

An individual with a preponderance of planets in mutable signs, whilst adapting easily to other people and situations, may lack direction and fulfilment (in the sense of accomplishment). A lack of mutability may indicate an inability to play a supportive role or synthesize experience.

People cannot always be classified as predominantly one element or quality. Sometimes the planets fall evenly into two or three elements, or two qualities can have equal emphasis. Ideally, this should indicate a well-balanced individual, but until the relative strengths of the planets and aspects have been established there is no guarantee of this.

To some extent the placing of the planets in the houses[5] may compensate for a missing element or quality, so that a person with

[5] See Appendix.

heavily tenanted air houses (3rd, 7th, and 11th) may thus offset their lack of planets in air signs. But greater emphasis should be placed on the elements and qualities as indicated by the signs than the houses as far as synastry is concerned. Certainly the combinations of the cross elements and qualities is immediately apparent in the workings of a relationship. Far from the ideal of fire mating with air, one finds that the antipathetical elements and qualities gravitate to each other.

Fire/Fire

Initially, couples having a strong emphasis in the same element would seem to be ideally suited; but when it comes to relationships, a better balance is achieved by a combination of different elements. However, there is much to be said for two people looking at the world from the same viewpoint. Fire/fire relationships, particularly with the same sign, can be wonderful at first as each one sees himself (or herself) reflected so perfectly in the other; but the long term outlook for this somewhat combustible team is less than rosy. Certainly the fire signs' fear of boredom is unlikely to manifest itself with this combination.

Aries, Sagittarius and Leo have a great capacity for falling in love (and out) easily and often. In fact life without romance of one sort or another is pretty bleak for the fire signs. Aries and Sagittarius need the excitement and thrill of 'pastures new' a little more than fixed Leo, who is more constant and likes permanence in his relationships. The fire/fire combination can be sexually exciting too as both individuals should share a lusty, inventive approach to sex. However, the danger of sudden attractions and the resultant jealousies and suspicions can ultimately undermine this partnership.

The double fire combination can be tremendously creative and productive, but without the caution and practicality of earth, for instance, two fiery types could find themselves in severe financial difficulties. The fire signs are notoriously extravagant and live for the moment; they also hate to be reminded of mundane responsibilities and obligations. Consequently they are all too often in the position of looking with hindsight at the benefits of insurance policies and pension schemes which they were too shortsighted to secure for themselves. This combination may get by in youth, when friendly bank managers and an understanding family are prepared to bail the couple out of their difficulties. But unless both partners mature and learn to control their impulsiveness and extravagance, each will blame the other for the resultant chaos when the problems begin to mount up and no one comes to the rescue.

One of the other drawbacks of fire/fire relationships is that both tend to prefer the driver's seat, so the less dominant partner is forced into a subordinate role which continually frustrates him or her. Eventually this one finds someone else and leaves, usually after an explosive plate-throwing scene. Fire needs careful tending for without fuel it will go out and with too much it will get out of control, leaving a trail of devastation.

Fire/Earth

Fire and earth are decidedly conflicting elements, both physically and symbolically. Too much earth will extinguish fire and too much fire scorches earth. Yet the combination of fire and earth in a relationship is not so unthinkable given some consideration. Although the values and behaviour of these elements are poles apart, they both benefit considerably from each other's abilities. In referring to the drawbacks of fire/fire combinations, fire's preference for living in the present and its indifference to restraint will soon be brought to terms by earth's religious adherence to practicalities. Thus Aries is drawn to Capricorn; Leo to Taurus; and Sagittarius to Virgo; for the attraction of similar qualities yet essentially antithetical elements acts like a magnet.

Zip Dobyns in *Finding the Person in the Horoscope* refers to the fire/earth combination as the 'steam-roller', for the combination of fire's irrestible force and optimism and earth's tenacity, strategy and realism are exceedingly productive and powerful. In the early stages of a relationship between these two elements, fire will be drawn to the strength, reserve and consistence of earth, whilst earth will be attracted to the happy, confident, charismatic quality of fire. In the beginning, too, fire will curb his own extravagance and cajole earth out of his depressions; likewise earth will splash out with the odd evening's entertainment and tolerate fire's childish whims and mistakes. But there comes a point when fire becomes exasperated with earth's discipline and plodding cautious pace and earth is no longer prepared to accept fire's irresponsibility and impulsiveness.

Sometimes the sexual interaction of fire and earth produces difficulties too. Apart from the initial attraction, which can be dynamic to say the least, earth may find fire a little aggressive and unorthodox in his approach and fire may find earth a little dull and unimpressed with the erotic and the unusual.[6]

[6] Strong Moon, Venus, Mars and Uranus, Neptune contacts will counteract this tendency in a predominantly earthy chart.

The critical point at which the overwhelming differences between the two signs must be faced is inevitably reached by all earth/fire combinations, but the result depends on the course of action then taken. Fire must recognize the importance of reality and foresight, cease to expect earth to deal with all the humdrum practicalities of life, and begin to contribute as well. Earth needs to find his inner vision and basic good will and instead of remaining stoically in a rut of routine and security, act spontaneously and take the occasional risk. Should the two remain convinced that their own approach is the only right one and are unable to change each other, they will move further and further apart, fire becoming increasingly icy and earth increasingly surly. Should the two adopt the 'higher path', however, the earth/fire combination can move on to a new level of mutual support and achievement. But it takes considerable effort, self-awareness and compromise.

Fire/Air

Fire and air are a good combination in relationships. Both these elements dislike pessimism and cautious thinking; they enjoy social interaction, entertainment and the creation of new ideas. Air can analyze the probable outcome of fire's action without squashing its enthusiasm; but since air touches lightly on things and fire is rather heavy-handed, air can waft gently away when the difficulties arise (claiming its usual impartiality), leaving fire to answer for the consequences. Fire stimulates air to get his ideas off the ground, as sometimes air hovers between two or three possibilities, and needs fire to provide the vital incentive to make a decision.

With fire and air combinations, the opposition (180° aspect) is brought into focus through the quadruplicities, providing some interesting 'sparks'. Polarities are always present in astrology and they embody a principle expressed by Jung that every idea contains the seed of its opposite. Thus behind every Aries protagonist hides a diplomatic Libra; in every self-glorifying Leo lurks a humanitarian Aquarian; and contained within every high-minded Sagittarian is a logical Gemini.

Although the qualities of rational thought and intuitive action seem an entirely satisfactory blend, these two elements sometimes lack substance and in the long term each partner may feel he or she has never really come to grips with the other. Initially fire will be drawn to air's versatile mind and witty repartee and air will be attracted to fire's warmth and direction. These two elements continue to support each other throughout a relationship and because neither bears long-term grudges, they survive the odd squabble and disagreement. The sexual relationship, too, is usually satisfactory, as fire and air share a liking for fantasy and erotica, and with air's agile imagination and fire's lusty response there are likely to be few problems. Occasionally, fire can feel air is a shade too aesthetic and intellectual about love and air can feel that fire is a little impatient and indiscriminating; but unless there are Moon, Venus, Mars and Saturn cross-afflictions, all should be well.

If there are any major drawbacks to this combination, it rests with air's usual problems in relating to its feelings, in contrast with fire's high emotional level and passionate desires. Although these two elements may be able to communicate well with each other, air cannot sustain a 'grande passion' and fire cannot remain detached from its feelings for too long. However the differences here are more resolvable than those of fire/earth or fire/water; even if it means each person doing his own thing to a certain degree.

Fire/Water

With the combinations discussed so far, the differences between the elements, whilst not always easy, are at least accessible as they involve characteristics that can be modified; indeed earth and air offer a degree of control and perspective to fire. However, fire and water make uneasy sleeping partners in every sense. Both these signs are highly emotional, but in entirely different ways. Fire is hot-blooded and spontaneous and the emotions are directed outwards, not necessarily requiring a response. Water, a passive and more yielding element needs emotional nourishment and understanding, and although the emotions are not exactly directed inwards, the water signs do need a response. The fire signs are apt to be thoughtless and self-centred but they forgive and forget easily; the water signs are highly sensitive and vulnerable and tend to brood and sulk when hurt. Fire frequently becomes exasperated with water's inability to snap out of his moods, and water feels fire is unsympathetic and selfish. Consequently the dialogue between these two elements is fraught with problems.

Fire does not mean to tread on water's toes or intentionally hurt him, but because water is reluctant to speak of his grievances (for fear of being hurt even more) emotional tension builds up between them. When the flood gates of water's emotions finally burst, instead of evoking compassion in fire, the reverse may happen, as fire is rendered immobile by water's over-emotional display.

Thus, the major problem facing the fire/water combination is in accepting their different emotional needs and behaviour and accommodating each other. In some ways the fire partner has to work the harder of the two, as he has constantly to take into account water's excessive vulnerability; water has to overcome his tendency to suffer in silence, whilst building up huge grudges which if left too long are impossible to overcome.

Here again the fire/water combinations in the same quadruplicity seem to have a fatal attraction for each other, so the Aries/Cancer; Leo/Scorpio; Sagittarius/Pisces couples are all too familiar to the astrologer.

The physical aspect of a fire/water relationship usually gets off to a good start, as fire is still watching his step and water has not begun yet to feel too vulnerable or offended. However, as the emotions run high with both these elements, large adjustments and condiserations have to be made for things to run smoothly. Water's sexual impulse is related to his feelings, so if he is feeling hurt or just moody, he is likely to be unresponsive sexually. Conversely, unless fire is ill, his sexual energy is easily ignited. Thus water often punishes fire for his errors by rejecting his advances, and so sex becomes quite a weapon between these two elements. With a good deal of understanding, fire and water can provide a loving, lasting bond with each other, which is important as both elements tend to be emotionally insecure. But as with the fire/earth combination, it takes some doing.

Earth/Earth

Although the earth/earth combination has none of the dramatic pitfalls of fire/fire, and certainly none of the financial or emotional ups and downs, it also has none of the excitement. The inclination of the earth signs is to play it safe and to stay with the familiar rather than venture into the unknown. The two signs together bring a good deal of mutual respect, support and security to each other's lives and whilst many of the other element combinations are busy separating, divorcing or re-marrying, this combination usually sustains a lifelong companionship. The dependability of the earth signs ensures that most aspects of life can be worked out on the basis of 'that which endures must be a worthwhile investment', and when disagreements occur, basic common sense usually unites them.

As this element is strongly physical, the sexual combination of earth/earth is normally satisfactory, although each is unlikely to discuss the other's emotional and physical needs (earth rarely questions the physical act). However, as the earth signs tend to suppress their emotional needs in favour of security, they are highly vulnerable to romantic attractions. Whilst they are unlikely to uphold infidelity or actively seek extra-marital relationships, the unconscious need for the unconventional and the novel tempts them to more exciting encounters. Nevertheless, earth/earth combinations are highly aware of their responsibility to each other and providing there are some more stimulating cross aspects between the two, the relationship should be durable and mutually satisfying.

Earth/Air

Air may be an essential ingredient in transporting the seeds that make earth fruitful, but it also generates a good deal of dust as well. Consequently earth/air relationships, like fire/water, can be difficult.

Earth usually finds air rather superficial and difficult to pin down, whereas air is stifled by earth's conservative and practical approach. For these reasons there is often little initial attraction between these two elements, but if a relationship is sparked off, this combination can be both productive and durable. Earth and air share one essential characteristic, and that is a rational mind; the difference is that air has an intellectual bias and tends to be theoretical, whilst earth prefers the strictly realistic and practical application of ideas. Nevertheless, with air's conceptual brilliance and earth's persistence and organization, these two elements can make tremendous headway in the world.

The real differences between the two elements emerge in the emotional/sexual area. Both elements have a tendency to isolate their feelings; air because he has difficulty in relating to them, and earth because he controls his emotions and sets great store by the physical act. Thus, air may feel the earthy partner lacks romance or refinement and is preoccupied with the body. By contrast, earth may be frustrated and perplexed by air's inability to respond to mere physical stimulation without fantasy and subtle innuendo. This is why the fire/earth combinations ultimately work better in a relationship such as marriage, where sex is an integral factor, whilst earth/air combinations do better in a working relationship, where sex and/or emotions are superfluous.

On the plus side, air stimulates earth's mental sluggishness and takes him 'out of himself'; earth brings air's flights of fancy into reality and gives him stability and substance. Again, this partnership, like fire/earth, needs an awareness of each other's temperamental differences to really succeed.

Earth/Water

The combination of these two sympathetic elements works well in a relationship. Earth's stability and dependability is a perfect foil for water's insecurity and vulnerability. Earth never feels hot and bothered as he does with fire, or ruffled and confused as he does with air. Water responds instinctively and undemandingly to earth, whilst earth is resiliant and steadfast. There are drawbacks, however, even with the best of combinations, and with earth and water, their mutual inclination towards doubt and pessimism is magnified when they get together. If earth is undergoing difficulties and water fears his security is threatened, neither will be able to boost the other's flagging confidence nor counter their neurotic tendencies. These two elements will withdraw further and further into themselves, driven by their own worries and negative thinking.[7]

The physical aspect of an earth/water relationship is usually good. Water feels instinctively 'at home' and safe with earth so that his emotional security releases his sexual expression. In return earth has a passive, responsive partner whose need for physical contact (strongly linked to his emotions) satisfies earth's physical desires.

With all element combinations, the understanding of each partner's temperamental differences is central to the success or failure of the relationship. Earth may have difficulty in rationalizing water's inconsistent moods and water may find earth a little overbearing and dogmatic; but on the whole, these two elements provide a good balance and this combination is mutually beneficial and durable.

Air/Air

With two predominantly airy partners, lack of communication between the two is never likely to be a problem, but there is a possibility of the relationship being rather cerebral, if not ultimately platonic. This can present problems if one partner has more earth and water in his chart, as he may feel the relationship is too lightweight and emotionally unsatisfying.

As discussed in the preceeding element, combinations of fire/fire and earth/earth, although the similarity of temperaments does have its benefits, the 'cons' tend to outweigh the 'pros' overall. Two airy people may be initially highly stimulated mentally by each other and have an enviable rapport; but as many of their ideas never get off the ground, in time both may accuse each other of being 'all talk and no action'.

[7] Obviously this tendency will be modified if both people have more positive aspects natally and in comparison.

This combination is exceedingly romantic. All three signs, Aquarius, Gemini and Libra, have a literary bent when it comes to love and great attention is spent on finding the right setting and atmosphere for love making itself. As both partners are less in touch with the physical senses, they need subtle methods and an element of fantasy to goad them into action.

Air/air couples usually have a good social life and pursue joint cultural and intellectual interests, and although they enjoy debate, they are less prone to petty domestic skirmishes than the other element combinations. As air is exceedingly restless, however, the air/air relationship may have its share of separations; but providing there is mutual agreement on the scale of their 'extra-mural activities', no lasting damage should be done by the occasional flirtation. Air couples are often considered to be ideally happy by onlookers, and indeed they often are.

Air/Water

Air and water are not the easiest of elements to combine in a relationship. Air is detached from its feelings whilst water is consumed by them. Yet air and water types are often fatally attracted to each other. Air is fascinated by water's intuitive feelings, his sensitivity and his reticence. Water admires air's social adroitness, his reasoning power and his mental agility.

The early stages of an air/water relationship can be entirely absorbing for both elements. Air will be attempting to unravel water's irrational moods and water will be captivated by air's brilliance and fascinating conversation. As both elements thrive on romance and subtle sexual manoeuvres, this duo is somewhat elusive and difficult to grasp, not only for everyone else but for the central characters themselves. Thus the 'courtship' for these two elements can be rather long and drawn out. After a period of time, however, the vastly different priorities of these two elements will begin to show.

Water needs understanding and stability to function at its best, and air is unlikely to provide either. He may try to reason with water but he usually fails to understand him, and the restlessness of air transmits itself all too easily to water, making him insecure. Air feels he is unable to circulate freely with water's possessive and clinging tendencies (no matter how subtle they may be). He is frustrated by trying to reason with water and, rather like fire, is rendered immobile by overwhelming emotional displays. This type of stalemate causes many air/water couples to 'throw in the towel'. Typically, the air partner usually admits defeat first, leaving water in his all too familiar role of the rejected lover.

To go back to the beginning of the chapter, in regard to the individual tendency to gravitate towards those who exemplify what he himself lacks, unless a person is highly self-aware he will eventually despise that which initially attracted him. In the air/water situation, air's fascination for the feeling quality of water all too often becomes criticism of the latter's over-emotional behaviour, and water's attraction for the reasoning and intellectual strength of air becomes a criticism of his callous and unfeeling treatment. With awareness, however, this combination can prove very fruitful, for air can modify water's oversensitivity and enable him to rationalize his experience and cope with the world at large, whereas water can show air the need for sensitivity to others and enrich his theoretical view of the world.

Water/Water

With two water signs in a relationship, lack of feeling and emotional distance is unlikely to be a problem. Indeed, it is quite the opposite, for their hypersensitivity to each other's feelings can overswamp the relationship. As with the other dual-element combinations, the reinforcement of the positive traits is all well and good, but the problems are multiplied when the more negative tendencies are duplicated. With two water signs the inclination to be oversensitive and fearful of confronting issues can lead to an 'us against the world' situation which is difficult to reverse. Water needs to distance itself from its emotions from time to time and with two emotional and sensitive people this is almost impossible. Although they can relate intuitively to each other, being compassionate and mutually comforting when things go wrong, they cling together instead of actively going out to meet the difficulty. As water is prone to developing all sorts of phobias, the symptoms are often exacerbated by misplaced sympathy and compounded worries.

This element fears rejection and isolation more than the others, so that the water signs tend to cling on to outworn relationships for the emotional security they provide. Thus with two water signs together, no matter how unsatisfying the relationship or how unhappy they may be, neither will be able to sever the connection. They tend instead to wait for circumstances to make the break for them, or else one will provoke the other into an emotional impasse, thus allowing 'him' to play the wronged and rejected party. Both tend to cling to the past and usually the nearest they come to admitting that things are wrong is in physical rejection and emotional coldness. Unless one partner has more air and fire, this sort of situation can linger on for years.

On the more positive side, this partnership has great depth of understanding and the ability to withstand all kinds of difficulties and setbacks. Two predominantly watery people can remain content with each other for the span of their lives, in apparently effortless symbiosis.

Largely conflicting element patterns between two people, in which, for instance, one is predominantly fire/air with a little earth and the other is mainly earth/water, can be problematic but they are by no means impossible to resolve. Likewise, too much similarity in the elements can produce some tension and conflict as well, as we have seen in the preceeding paragraphs. As far as the qualities are concerned, two very cardinal people can become overly aggressive, with ego-battles developing all too easily; predominantly mutable people may scatter their energies so wide that they move right away from each other; and too great a fixed emphasis in a couple may increase their obstinate tendencies and create many blocks between them. Contrasting, rather than conflicting, elements and qualities are most desirable in synastry.

2.
CASE STUDIES (I)

> We all have certain electric and magnetic powers within us and ourselves exercise an attractive and repelling force, according as we come into touch with something like or unlike.
>
> *Goethe*

In order to develop the idea of the way the elements and qualities can give an immediate idea of the dialogue between a couple, we shall look at the following charts and assess their interaction purely on that basis. Obviously there are many other important factors to be included in a full chart comparison, but these can be incorporated later.

Although the balance of the elements and qualities can be easily established by counting up the planets as they fall in each group, it is also necessary to take into account which planets are actually involved. If a personal planet (Sun, Moon, Mercury, Venus or Mars) is found in a particular element, this element will carry more weight in interpretation than if Uranus, Neptune and Pluto (or even Saturn and Jupiter) are found in this element. (As Uranus, Neptune and Pluto spend many years in a sign, they are considered less personal. However, their natal house position and aspects to them by the personal planets, draw them into individual experience.) The exception here is when one of these outer planets happens to be the ruler of the Ascendant and therefore the chart ruler. Thus, if an individual has three planets in water and one in fire, and the three happen to be Uranus, Neptune and Pluto and the one the Moon, despite the apparent weakness of fire, an astrologer would still expect the qualities associated with this element to overshadow those of water.

The charts (Figures 4 and 5) are those of a married couple who have been together for four years. The attraction between them was strong and immediate and despite many external challenges (financial and otherwise), the couple are happy and feel ideally suited. John and Mary are a good example of the 'steam roller'

Figure 4: John's chart.

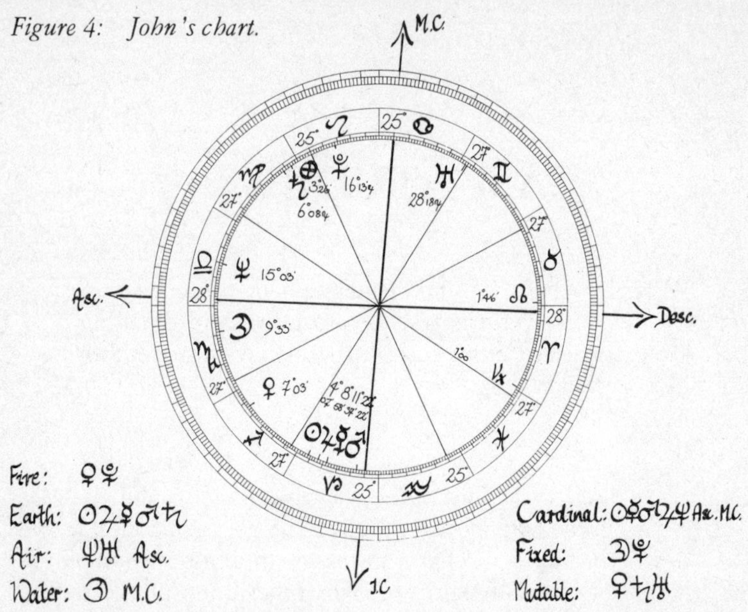

combination mentioned in the previous chapter, and as this can be difficult to handle their individual ability to accept each other for their differences, rather than try to change them, is a contributory factor to their happiness.

Mary is a fire/water type and has no planets whatsoever in earth signs (not even the Ascendant and Midheaven). John has a predominance in earth, with fire little emphasized. (Venus, although important as it is his Ascendant ruler, is the only *personal* planet in this element; as it is a feminine principle, it is more indicative of the type of woman he is seeking.[1]) Mary, as a fire/water type, is highly emotional and oscillates between impulsive action (fire) and sudden lapses of confidence (water).[2] Although highly creative, she needs stability and good management to realize her goals and the security of a permanent relationship to anchor her emotions. John is typical of earth, with the Sun, Mercury, Mars, Jupiter and Saturn in this element. He is responsible, cautious and constructive. He may be somewhat lacking in spontaneity and creativity, but he is ultimately likely to achieve his objectives. He needs inspiration and encouragement to get more enjoyment out of life and to ensure that success comes before they are too old to appreciate it. Thus he is

[1] See Chapter 4 (p. 56).

[2] This is magnified by Mars (Sun ruler) conjunct Saturn square the Ascendant.

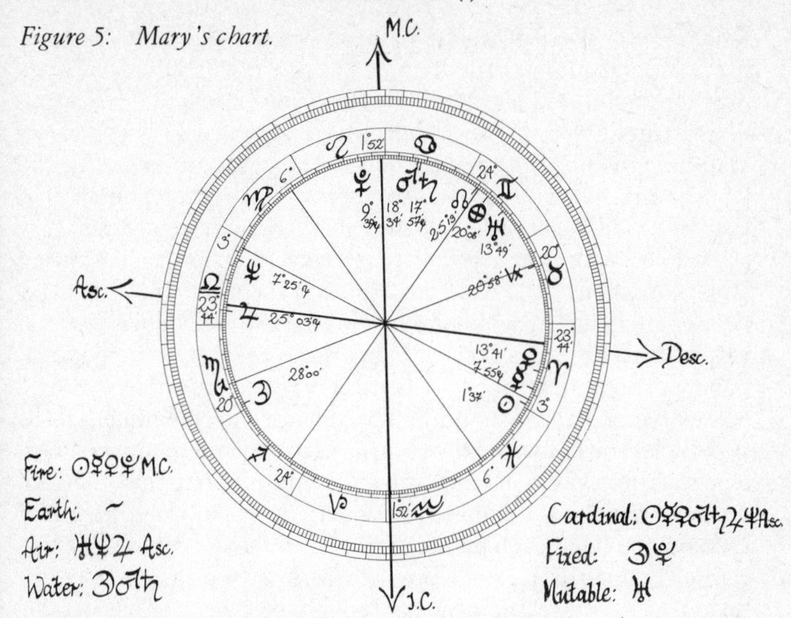

Figure 5: Mary's chart.

attracted to Mary's outgoing, positive personality.

John and Mary are predominantly cardinal so they are both achieving types and extremely self-assertive. These two charts are also indicative of the attraction between similar qualities yet antithetical elements—Mary has a strong Aries emphasis and John a predominance in Capricorn. As these two signs are highly ambitious, the combination of their energies is likely to get them the results they desire, at least in the world at large. In fact both have encouraged and helped each other to become more established in their respective careers. However, the strong personality clashes frequently stand in the way of the peace and harmony sought by their Libra Ascendants. They have entirely different modes of behaviour; Mary likes immediate action and quick results, whereas John prefers to take his time and the innate assertiveness of Aries and Capricorn can drive them both to distraction on occasion. Here the difference between the cardinal fire/water combination as opposed to the fixed or mutable one can be clearly seen. Although head-on collisions are bound to occur with similar qualities in a relationship, there is a preference for 'fighting it out' with the cardinals, rather than blocking or resisting like the fixed, or running around in ever decreasing circles like the mutable.

Both partners have no personal planets in air signs, which might initially signify communication problems and show an inability to detach themselves from heated situations. But even without looking at the detail of Mercury aspects, we can see that both people have Ascendants in air, which enable them to find an objective meeting point (albeit after the dust has settled). Since the Ascendants are in Libra, a sign identified with the principle of relating and fair-play, they both have the ability to give way and compromise when necessary. Another very important point here is that John and Mary each have the ruler of their Ascendant in a fire sign (with a wide trine aspect between each ruler), which is a strong and harmonious link. A further factor in their favour is that their Moons are in water signs, which helps the two individuals respond instinctively to each other and underlines their strong emotional bond. As both their Moon signs are Scorpio, the passions are deep, possessive and all-consuming. The relationship is unlikely to be superficial and both need the security of a deep and lasting relationship that involves total (and exclusive) commitment on both parts.

As outlined in the previous chapter, the pitfalls of a fire/earth relationship lie in each partner trying to force the other to be like himself, which is just not possible with two strong-minded individuals. As the relationship has brought both people considerable happiness, the inherent problems of this element combination are being handled well. In this case, the couple have many shared interests and similar values, but the overriding factor is a deep love for one another and open emotional lines between them. As with all relationships, time will be the real test.

The charts in Figures 6 and 7 are another good example of each partner supplying the lacking element in the other. Vivien Leigh and Sir Laurence Olivier were a fascinating, talented and glamorous couple. They had an exceedingly passionate and turbulent relationship that lasted twenty-three years. Both left spouses and children for each other in a haze of publicity in 1939, but the marriage finally ended in 1960.

Vivien Leigh was a predominantly air/water type. A closer examination of the planets concerned shows that the Moon and Venus are in air signs (both descriptive of her femininity) whilst the Sun and Mars, both masculine principles,[3] are in water. Both fire and earth are weak in Vivien's chart although Mercury, a personal planet, is in Sagittarius. Olivier, on the other hand, has at first glance a predominantly earth/water chart, but as Neptune, Saturn and Jupiter are the planets in water and the Sun, Mercury, Mars and the Moon in earth, the latter element really predominates. Air

[3] See Chapter 4 (pp. 51, 58).

Figure 6: Laurence Olivier's chart.

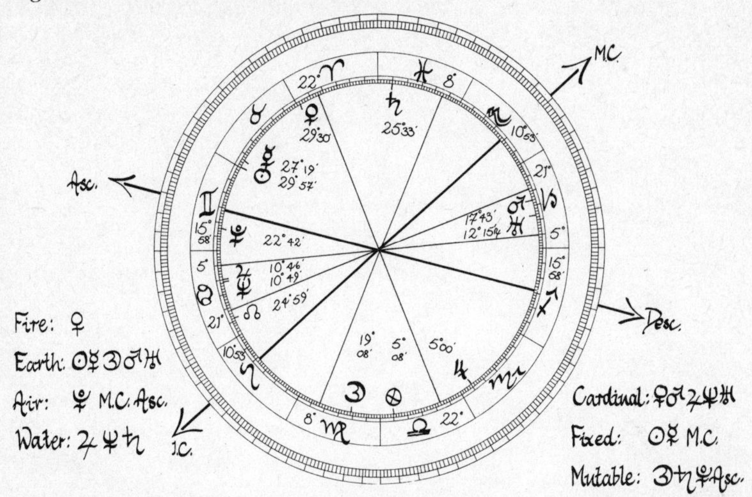

and fire look weak in Olivier's chart; firstly, Pluto is the only planet in air, but as the Ascendant and Midheaven are in Gemini and Aquarius respectively, this element is brought right into focus. Olivier's Venus is his one fire planet and as this is thirty minutes away from the sign of Taurus, and by progression would have occupied this sign for nearly thirty years of his life, fire in real terms is little featured in his chart. Thus Olivier is primarily an earth/air type.

Vivien Leigh was very illustrative of the air/water combination. She was passionate and vulnerable (water); both these qualities came through her screen portrayals, yet the quick intelligence and flirtatious quality of air was also present. Unfortunately, this combination can have its pitfalls, as it indicates a delicate balance between the intellect and the emotions — reality and fantasy. Vivien was in fact manic-depressive and spent her latter years in and out of nursing homes. Perhaps the notorious insecurity of 'show business' exacerbated her sensitive psychological constitution. Vivien Leigh, like Mary in the first combination, needed emotional security and stability in her life. In a way, Olivier became a sort of Svengali figure for her, moulding her beauty and talent into a fine theatrical vehicle. However, as their careers and differences drove them apart, her insecurities and fears deepened. She alternated between periods of calmness and objectivity and hysterical obsessional behaviour. In many ways, the more she clamoured for emotional reassurance, the further she drove Olivier away.

Figure 7: Vivien Leigh's chart.

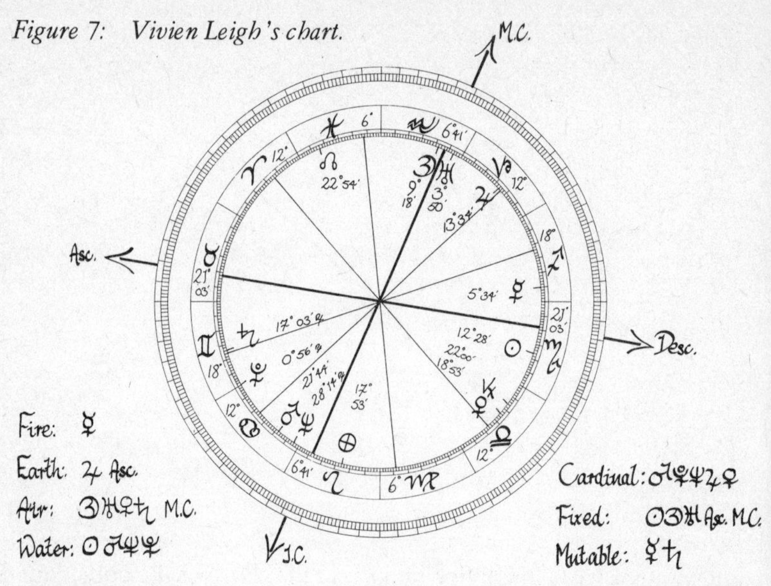

Olivier, one of the world's greatest actors, has shown the strength of earth by remaining at the top of his profession for fifty years, not only performing, but producing, directing and managing a theatre company. Here, too, one can see the air emphasis represented in his need for intellectual challenge and in his ability to play a multiplicity of roles (especially typical of his Gemini Ascendant). Although he is reluctant to discuss his marriage to Vivien, there is little doubt that their relationship (at least in the early stages) was an exceedingly passionate one. The Taurus/ Scorpio polarity of their Suns is one of the indicators of an all or nothing approach to life and of course the attraction of opposites. As both Suns are in fixed signs, it would be difficult for them to give way to each other over points about which they felt very strongly.

Olivier would have been attracted to Vivien not only for her great beauty but for her passion and sensitivity (water) and her mental agility (air). She would have challenged his views and provided a mentally stimulating and emotionally responsive partner. However, although her personality changes may have captivated him at first, they could have alarmed and drained him as they got more and more out of control. Vivien would have been attracted to Olivier's talent, control and his strong physical sense (earth), but as the relationship progressed and he became less responsive to her emotional ups and downs, she may have accused him of insensitivity (lack of water).

The Ascendants are also a good indicator of the cross element currents between them. Vivien's Ascendant in earth ties up with Olivier's Taurus emphasis; Venus, her Ascendant ruler, however, is in Libra, an air sign. The same thing happens in Olivier's chart. The Ascendant is in air, but Mercury, the ruler, is in earthy Taurus. On balance we can see there is a strong earth/air relationship which neatly mirrored Olivier's natal picture. Yet despite the love they had for each other, the relationship deteriorated, although by today's standards twenty-three years is a long time. Perhaps we can see the underlying problem lay in the inability to integrate the water side of their relationship.

Vivien's Sun and Mars in water show that she needed an understanding, feeling man to relate to as a partner. Olivier, as primarily earth/air, may have given her stability, but he could only apply his rational mind when confronted by an emotional display. In the early stages, the relationship would have been carried by the strong physical passion between them. But over the years the lack of real emotional response in him undermined her sensitive psychological structure. Although he may not have been the root cause of her mental problems, no doubt the unhappiness she experienced in their relationship could have tipped the balance. Olivier's need for a peaceful supportive relationship became increasingly important over the years, and he subsequently married the actress Joan Plowright, strangely enough another Sun Scorpio, but with her Moon in the same earth sign as Olivier's — Virgo. Perhaps if Vivien's Moon had at least been in a compatible element, the story might have been different.

The third couple in Figures 8 and 9 are not so much illustrative of the supply and demand aspect of element interchange as of a combined lack of one particular element.

Much is documented about Adolf Hitler's rise to power and his subsequent abuse of it. We are aware of the effect he had on the German people in the 1930s, and of course on the destiny of the whole world. However, as far as his private life is concerned there is much conjecture, particularly over his relationship with Eva Braun. Eva was only seventeen when she met Adolf Hitler, who was nearly twice her age. Their relationship was conducted largely in secret, a factor which suited him, but not Eva, who disliked the anonymity of her position. Some sources maintain that there was no physical consummation of their relationship, whilst others suggest there was even a child. Hitler married Braun on the eve of their suicide in the bunker of a besieged Berlin, at the close of the war in 1945.

Eva Braun and Adolf Hitler were both fire/earth types. Hitler

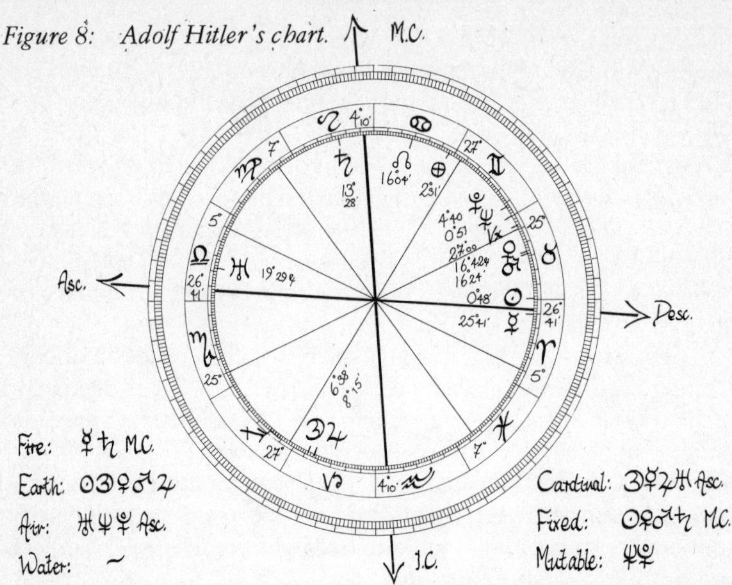

Figure 8: Adolf Hitler's chart.

was predominantly earthy (Sun, Moon, Venus, Mars and Jupiter in earth) as his air planets are Uranus, Neptune and Pluto, leaving only the Ascendant in Libra. Their Suns follow the pattern already seen in the other two examples of similar qualities (fixed) but antithetical elements (air, earth). Eva Braun had Sun, Mars, Uranus and Pluto in air, the two outer planets lending weight on this occasion, as Uranus is the Sun's ruler and Pluto that of the Ascendant. Eva's Moon, Venus, Mercury and Saturn were all in earth signs, so there is a fairly even balance between air and earth in her chart. What they both lacked was water. Hitler had no planets whatsoever in this element and Eva had only Neptune, although the Ascendant was in Scorpio.

Certainly on Hitler's side we can see how the lack of water manifested itself in his behaviour. Firstly, he had a theoretical image of how the world should be (air) and a fanatical and extreme approach (fixed) to achieving it (earth). His apparent insensitivity to people's feelings on a mass scale speaks for itself, and although he was exceedingly sentimental he displayed considerable lack of sensitivity in his dealings with colleagues and those closest to him. Charm he had, but feelings themselves were apparently lacking. Whenever his feelings did assert themselves, they erupted in an irrational outburst that he seemed unable to control. His views on women were somewhat chauvinistic: he was quoted as saying 'A man has to stamp his imprint on any woman', and he also maintained that 'women are not suited to politics because of their inability to

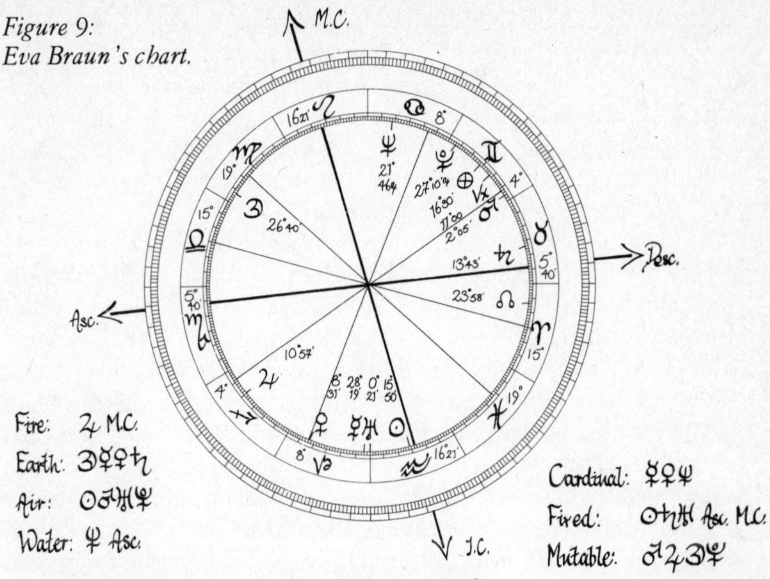

Figure 9: Eva Braun's chart.

discriminate between reason and emotion'.

Yet Hitler himself was considered to have exceedingly feminine characteristics. Some even think he was a homosexual. He had an obsession about wearing gloves, his voice became high, almost falsetto, when angry or excited and he even used to offer to do his officers' washing for them. Because water, as represented by the feminine signs, was lacking in his horoscope, he was completely out of touch with this aspect of his psyche. Unable to integrate this principle successfully into his personality, it presented itself as a crude caricature of femininity.

Eva we know less about. From her chart it appears that as an airy Aquarius she was able to cope with her unconventional position as Hitler's mistress and hold out (earth) until she got her man, providing she was recognized — and for this she was even prepared to die. But here too it seems as though her emotions were uncoordinated and largely attention seeking. She attempted suicide twice over her unacknowledged and neglected position and indeed after the second attempt Hitler installed her in a villa, thus placating her and officially establishing her as his mistress. Although she became more actively involved in Hitler's life after this, he refused to marry her and according to some authorities probably never would have done, even if the war had gone another way. As far as marriage was concerned, Hitler had a rather romanticized view of things: 'A woman who loves her husband lives for him alone . . . Thus she demands that he in turn live for her.

Marriage would have been a terrible burden to take on.'

There are, of course, many inter-aspects and important contacts between Eva and Hitler's chart, not to mention their own problematical natal configurations. But in broad terms, their individual and combined earth/air mixture shows that both of them could tolerate an emotionally unsatisfactory relationship, providing they had physical contact and communication.

It is unlikely that their relationship was unconsummated. Despite Hitler's apparent emotional atrophy, his earth emphasis indicates a need for physical gratification. That he had other mistresses (with whom, incidentally, punishment was an integral aspect of sexual pleasure[4]) is well documented, so it is unlikely that he would have carried on a platonic relationship to the degree of involvement that he did with Eva. Eva must have had a special something, however, particularly as Hitler endeavoured to keep their relationship private and entirely separate from his political life when in many ways a marriage to the perfect Aryan female might have been advantageous to him. Hitler avoided mature emotional relationships and seemed better able to relate to young naive females.[5] Eva for her part probably saw Hitler as an established, successful man and as she had an interest in politics prior to meeting him, the 'New World Leader' image cannot be ruled out of her attraction for him either. It must also be added that Eva's need for a father-figure is vividly descriptive of her seventh house Saturn, which will be discussed later in the book. Furthermore, Eva's own inexperience of the world would have prevented her from recognizing Hitler's psychological problems or peculiar sexual inclinations.

Although both no doubt experienced difficulty in expressing their emotions easily and well, their relationship mirrored their emotional requirements and gave stability and meaning to their lives. Hitler was committed to his world conquest and leadership and reluctant to take on a marriage with all its emotional ramifications. Perhaps his alleged homosexuality acted subconsciously to prevent his being able to make such an emotional commitment. For Eva, remembering that she had some water in her chart, there may have been a real commitment, yet her inexperience gave her nothing with which to compare their relationship. In a strange way their combined deficiencies and neurotic tendencies bonded them just as well as 'grande passion' and emotional sensitivity might

[4] Venus conjunct Mars square Saturn.

[5] He also had a relationship with his young niece Geli.

have done. One can only speculate on how world history might have been changed had Hitler's fanatical drive been softened in an emotionally satisfying family life.

3.
THE PLANETS, THE ANGLES AND THE SEVENTH HOUSE

> The fascination exerted by one human being over another is not what he emits from his personality at the present instant of encounter, but a summation of his entire being.
>
> *Anais Nin*

In the Introduction the importance of the individual becoming aware of his own contribution to the success or failure of his relationships through self-discovery was outlined. With this in mind, a relationship between two people can, therefore, really only be judged after each individual chart has been examined.

The sheer amount and variety of information that can be gleaned from a horoscopic circle containing ten planetary bodies is staggering; and indeed much depends on the level at which the interpretation is pitched. The horoscope is after all a 'photograph' of an actual moment in time taken from the point of view of the individual on Earth. Although the planets are living energies and have a physical reality, they appear in the birth chart as symbols. The essence of a symbol is its ability to express simultaneously the various aspects of the idea it represents. Unfortunately, much of the essence is lost in 'translation'.

Many esoteric thinkers, including Gurdjieff, Steiner and Edgar Cayce, maintain that we visit the planets after death, absorbing their natures as dimensions of consciousness. Upon returning to Earth, our experience is 'recorded' in symbolic form in the birth chart. Thus it is entirely possible that the meanings of the planets are perceived by each of us in our own unique way through our own individual experience. By the raising of consciousness, esoteric systems teach that one can become more in touch with these archetypal ideas.

Within the horoscopic symbolism we have a map of cosmic dimensions, a map that shows our heredity, our talents, our psychological structure and our potential. It is also a map that shows us our links with other people, and although we may not always understand the reasons behind these links, we can see how we attract certain experiences and people into our lives.

The horoscope comprises twelve houses, ten planetary bodies and two major axes, that of the Ascendant/Descendant and that of the Midheaven (M.C.)/Imum Coeli (I.C.). These two axes also provide the four angles, which are exceedingly important and sensitive in synastry. The houses 'influence' the 'action' of the planets in a natal chart. Although the fifth and eleventh houses are connected with romance and friendship respectively, for the purposes of this book we shall be concentrating on the meaning of the seventh house and, of course, on the planets and the angles.

A word here must be included about aspects. Through the angular relationships (aspects) that are formed between the planets, we gain a considerable amount of information about the quality of individual experience expressed by the planets. The major (harmonious) aspects that indicate comparative ease of expression are the sextile (60°), trine (120°) and the quintile (72°), and to a lesser extent the biquintile (144°). The major (inharmonious) aspects which require considerable effort to resolve and often indicate difficulties are the square (90°), the quincunx (150°), the opposition (180°) — although this can be a tremendously creative aspect depending on the planets concerned — and to a lesser extent the semi-square (45°), and the sesqui-quadrate (135°). The conjunction (when two planets lie on or near the same degree) is the most powerful aspect, involving the close merging of two principles, and can be harmonious or conflicting depending on the planets concerned. Finally, the semi-sextile (30°) aspect has been treated traditionally as an easy aspect. However, this aspect with its thirty-degree span is the equivalent of an entire sign, and on the basis that each consecutive sign has vastly different and conflicting properties from its predecessor, the semi-sextile really needs to be considered as inharmonious.[1]

The Ascendant/Descendant M.C./I.C. and the Seventh House

The horizontal Ascendant/Descendant axis cuts the horoscopic circle in half; the lower hemisphere (marking the period of time during which the Sun is below the horizon) is considered to be the unconscious, subjective hemisphere, whilst the upper hemisphere (marking the daylight hours) is considered objective, and conscious. The Ascendant itself is the point where the unconscious

[1] For a deeper understanding of aspects, the reader should read an astrological text book. (See Recommended Reading in Appendix, p. 158.)

becomes conscious and indeed, in more spiritual terms, it can be seen as the point where the soul incarnates into the Earth plane. Consequently, the Ascendant is the most personal and sensitive point in the chart. The first house which follows on from the Ascendant degree describes the way we present ourselves to the world; it represents our mask — our persona. Directly opposite falls the Descendant, which likewise indicates the beginning of the seventh house. The latter describes how we experience other people and what we expect (often unconsciously) and receive in our relationships. This house is also known as the house of open enemies, and as such shows the traps we make for ourselves in the expectations of our relationships and our contribution to them.

We make a terrible mistake, however, if we assume that the seventh house in a natal chart is only indicative of other people's effect on the individual. The horoscope is descriptive of each person's totality and everything, including all the houses and all the planets, reflects facets of the individual's inner and outer life. The aim of the individual should be to integrate harmoniously all aspects of himself (or herself). As the seventh house is specifically concerned with one-to-one relationships, this area offers the opportunity of making conscious otherwise hidden facets of our personality and uniting them.

Of course it is exceedingly difficult to be conscious of everything we are and all too often unconscious energies are projected on to others. As the Descendant and seventh house are opposite to the area of highest self-awareness (Ascendant), whilst not exactly representing the lowest point, this area tends to be ripe for all kinds of projection. Occasionally the partner is vividly portrayed by the seventh house (the sign on the Descendant being that of the partner's Sun, possibly even conjunct the Sun itself). However, if, for instance, Uranus is placed in the seventh house and the individual is married, but neither to an Aquarian nor to a strongly Uranian person, then this placement is expressing the individual's need for freedom in his relationships and the likelihood that the partner is a free spirit.

The combination of planets found in the seventh house and the sign(s) they occupy describe the quality of the relationships we are seeking and the people we are likely to attract in order to experience that outlined potential. The aspects to those planets indicate the ease or difficulty involved in relating to others and in achieving harmony and fulfilment in partnerships. Sometimes no planet at all appears in the seventh house, which does not mean that the individual has no relationships or even that they are unimportant to him. In this case, in order to explore this area, we have to look to the position of the ruler of the sign on the seventh house cusp and its aspects.

Although the seventh house is traditionally the area concerned with one-to-one relationships, the eighth house too has a part to play here. This house, as a continuation from the seventh, and in opposition to the second, is indicative of what one receives from relationships. Of course, this can mean financial benefits (hence the idea of inheritance associated with the eighth house) and 'other people's money' (as opposed to that received through one's own efforts, designated by the second house). The eighth house has Scorpio/Pluto rulership and is synonymous with the hidden aspects of life — death and rebirth, transformation. It also has much to do with sexual matters (usually something experienced in marriage). In as much as the second house involves feelings and possessions, the eighth house represents the feelings and possessions relating to partnerships. One can observe what happens when feelings get betrayed in a relationship, in the acrimonious bartering of shared possessions! So planets in the eighth house can be exceedingly revealing when it comes to relationships, and should be noted carefully. In fact a planet in the eighth house can be used to give guidance in relationship matters in the absence of any seventh house planets.

Taking the horoscope as representative of the totality of the individual, there is an interesting link with a myth describing the celestial origin of man. According to Plato in the *Timaeus*, the first men were androgynous (having both male and female characteristics in the same body) with four arms and legs. They were incredibly powerful but their growing superiority threatened the gods, who split them in two. Thus each half spent its life searching for the other, leaving the gods to their own devices. This is very much akin to the idea of a soul mate or the perfect balance and harmony man is seeking, which in fact is part of himself.

A great many people hope that they *will* find their twin soul (particularly those with Neptune-ruled Ascendants or Descendants) and sometimes, very occasionally, they do. But in the main a lot of individual 'soul-searching' has to go on in pursuit of the ideal partnership!

The Ascendant and Descendant points are of major importance in chart comparison. One person's planets contacting the Ascendant or Descendant of another's chart is focusing on the most sensitive and personal part of the individual. Without some contact from one or both Ascendants or Descendants, the relationship is unlikely to proceed very far or to be exceedingly significant. Indeed, this axis is usually the prime mover in the initial attraction of one partner to another. (In my own personal experience, when I have been at a social gathering, I often feel particularly drawn to an individual — we seem 'to hit it off'. Invariably, I later discover that the person has contacts to my Ascendant or Descendant or vice versa). If there are no aspects to this axis or the rulers of the Ascendant or Descendant, the Midheaven or Imum Coeli should be involved in some way.

Little is mentioned about the M.C./I.C. axis in synastry, yet in my own work I have found many couples with strong Midheaven and I.C. contacts. The M.C. as the cusp of the tenth house is descriptive, not just of our aims and ambitions in a professional sense, but of our pursuit of an ideal image of ourselves. So often our choice of relationships is coloured by what we hope the relationship will do for us in reflecting our ideals. Thus, it is entirely possible that if someone's planets affect our M.C. we hope they will do the work for us, feeling we may not have the ability ourselves. On the other hand many partnerships with strong M.C. contacts are those in which one partner is particularly helpful (or detrimental, depending on the planets and aspects concerned) to the other's career.

The M.C./I.C. axis can also be seen to represent the parents. The M.C., with its Saturn connection indicates the control and conditioning instilled in us by our parents (usually the more influential and dominant parent) that is instrumental in forming our ambitions. The I.C., with its lunar associations, indicates our instinctive sense of belonging to our parents and the formation of our emotional patterns (usually encouraged by the parent who provides the source of unconditional love and support). Thus the ease or difficulty encountered in relating to parental influence (as shown by the M.C./I.C. axis) is often reflected in later emotional relationships in adulthood. So the search for a parental figure can often be seen in M.C./I.C. contacts between a couple. As the M.C. falls in the upper hemisphere (conscious, objective) and the I.C. in the lower (unconscious, subjective), contacts to the I.C. are acutely sensitive and fundamental to the individual's emotional pattern.

Obviously, if an aspect is formed with the M.C., the I.C. is drawn in as well, thus a conjunction to the M.C. becomes an opposition to the I.C.; a sextile to the M.C. becomes a trine to the I.C. As with the Ascendant and Descendant, the first is highly self-aware, whilst the second is more unconscious.

Another good indication of a significant relationship is where there is an interplay between a couple's M.C./I.C. and Ascendant/

Descendant axis — one partner's Ascendant/Descendant axis reflecting (by interchange) the M.C./I.C. axis of the other. The angles forming the cross on which the horoscopic circle pivots are supremely important in synastry; unless these points are involved in chart comparison the relationship is unlikely to be deeply meaningful for the partners. In fact, the four angles of the horoscope can be likened to a tree, the M.C. representing those branches that reach out into infinity, the I.C., the roots that go deep into the earth and the Ascendant and Descendant, the horizontal branches that give balance and accessibility.

The Sun

The Sun in a chart represents our self-expression and the urge to create an identity. Yet so often in conveying the Sun sign characteristics in popular terms one actually loses sight of the real solar principle. In as much as the Sun is the centre of our solar system, sustaining and illuminating the planets, in a horoscope, the Sun symbolizes our basic motivating force — our *modus operandi*. The position of the Sun (by sign, house and aspects) colours the way we relate to all the other planetary principles. Each individual releases the Sun potential in every aspect of his life, yet the involvement of all the other planets makes the self-expression subtly different to each individual. The Sun in astrological symbolism shows us the greatest potential we possess and in effect its placing in each sign indicates the need to express our basic nature as creatively as possible.

Early man recognized the Sun as the source of all life and worshipped it as a god. It became the Great Father, the Great Hero. Indeed the Sun is very much the masculine principle in astrology, symbolizing the father, husband and all masculine ideas. Consequently, in a man's chart it is usually more consciously expressed. A man is aware at a relatively early age of the need to assert his dominance, whereas a woman may prefer to adopt a more submissive role, thereby finding her full identity in a relationship reflecting the characteristics of the male partner. Thus the Sun in a woman's chart is often projected through the man in her life as he (consciously) expresses what she (unconsciously) chooses not to do. Of course in these days of female emanicipation, women are living less vicariously. Many are now taking up the challenge of a stimulating career and are thus beginning to express their solar 'energy' in their own active and dynamic way.

The Sun's placing in a woman's chart can give the astrologer a good idea of the qualities she is seeking in a man. Although it is not as simple as to suggest that, for instance, every Aries female needs an Aries male to fulfil her Sun sign potential, it is nonetheless true that the principles symbolized by, in this case, the Sun in Aries, represent dominant qualities she seeks in a male.

The Sun in the Seventh House

When the Sun is found in the seventh house, the individual may place a tremendous amount of importance on relationships. His or her self-expression may flourish through relating to others, although if other factors indicate a basically insecure nature, he or she may only reflect other people's opinions and personality traits — this is the classic position for projecting one's own qualities on to others. Many traditional astrology books suggest that a seventh house Sun indicates that the 'native should make a successful marriage'. Not everyone with a seventh house Sun marries, however, and even if they do it is not always successful. Certainly the Sun here suggests that there is a basic drive to find a partner to balance the individual and that until this is found, his or her life will feel incomplete. But contrary to some opinions that the Sun here bodes well for a good marriage, because there is a tendency to seek perfection in relationships, this may mean that there are several one-to-one encounters (not necessarily marriage) before the right partner appears. (This is especially true if there are Uranus aspects to the Sun, Moon or Venus.)

The person with a seventh house Sun is likely to extol the value and importance of relating and of seeking harmony in relationships. Although they themselves may not marry, they may work in the counselling professions or actively seek to bring people together.

If the Sun is rising in a birth chart (conjunct the Ascendant or in the first house) it indicates that the individual has a dynamic personality, whereas if the Sun is setting (conjunct the Descendant and in the seventh house) the individual is more likely to be drawn to strong personalities. In this case, after a period of time, he or she may begin to realize that life is rather frustrating living in someone else's shadow and difficulties begin to emerge. The individual needs to be aware of his own potential and instead of allowing the partner to overshadow him (or her) assert his (or her) own individuality. Sometimes in realizing this, the pendulum can swing to the opposite extreme, making the individual determined to have his own way at any cost in order to even things out. With a seventh house Sun, there is a need to share 'centre stage', to compromise and to complement. In fact, this position of the Sun indicates the ability to acquire the real Libran balance in relationships.

The Moon

Opposites are present in all aspects of astrology, as indeed they are in life. We can see the Ascendant/Descendant and M.C./I.C. axes as polar opposites and with the planets too there are pairs of opposite 'energies'. The Sun and Moon are one such pair, in fact they represent the male/female principle itself and as such are the most important planets for consideration in a natal chart. Stephen Arroyo in his book *Astrology, Karma and Transformation* makes the interesting point that, viewed from the Earth, the Sun and Moon are identical in size, which is symbolic of the equal importance these two bodies should have in our lives.

Ancient Man worshipped the Moon as a goddess (usually of fertility): she was the archetypal feminine principle — the Great Mother. The changing face of the Moon became synonymous with woman's fluctuating emotions and inconsistent behaviour (reflecting her monthly cycle). In interpretation, the Moon's influence in the birth chart represents the emotions, the unconscious response, and femine figures such as mother and wife. It also represents the past, our origins and the way we act instinctively without having to rationalize.

As the Moon symbolizes the feminine principle it tends to be more to the forefront in a woman's nature than the Sun (as we have seen in the previous section). In fact, I find a lot of women are certainly more typical of their Moon sign than that of the Sun. In a man's chart, however, the Moon's influence may be overshadowed by the Sun's expression, so many of his lunar characteristics will be more descriptive of the women in his life, particularly his mother, but also his wife.

The Sun and Moon in a chart represent, respectively, the outer and inner being of the individual. It could also be said that the Sun (conscious self-expression) shows us 'where we are going' and the Moon (unconscious soul-expression) 'where we have come from'. The contact between the Sun and the Moon is therefore exceedingly important in astrology, whether in regard to a natal chart or chart comparison. Harmonious signs and aspects indicate an easy blending of these two ideas, whereas conflicting signs and aspects show that much effort is needed by the individual to create a happy balance in his own nature. Consequently, if an individual cannot unite these two principles in his own (inner) nature, he is going to have some difficulty in doing so in an (outer) marriage. A harmonious aspect between the Sun and the Moon (particularly when they are in compatible signs) can override otherwise difficult aspects in a chart. This does not mean that the other difficult aspects are rendered null and void but that the individual has a much better chance of ultimately finding equilibrium in his life. The Sun/Moon relationship is indicative of the individual's experience of mother and father who are strong models to be imitated in his (or her) own male/female interaction. Thus if the individual has a constructive experience of his mother and father, seeing them as balanced, supportive people (even if they are separated), it aids his chances of forming more successful adult relationships.

The Moon in the Seventh House

Individuals with a seventh house Moon are seeking emotional security in relationships. They expect unconditional love and acceptance, yet they frequently attract partners who play on their emotions and tend to smother and over-protect them. As the Moon symbolizes the mother (amongst other things), individuals with a seventh house Moon are drawn to relationships where they can be mothered or do the mothering themselves — sometimes a little of both.

The seventh house Moon can be a rather complex placing. On the one hand, if the Moon is well aspected, the individual is likely to have emotionally satisfying relationships, but if it forms difficult aspects, the individual may experience much heartache, upheaval and change in this area of life. Because of the inconsistent nature of the Moon itself, however, relationships may always seem to be in a state of flux and subject to all sorts of emotional ebbs and flows. As the seventh house is an area where considerable projection tends to occur, the Moon (representing instinctive unconscious patterns) can make the individual feel that he never seems to be in control of his relationships.

Individuals with the Moon here invariably want to marry young. However, if the Moon has some difficult aspects, delays and reluctance to enter emotional relationships may be more the case. Sometimes this reaction is connected with an adverse experience in childhood or emotional problems with mother.

On the positive side, a seventh house Moon indicates that the individual should have great perception and sensitivity towards other people's moods and feelings, which in the main is a fine feature for close relationships.

Mercury

Mercury is a planet all too easily underrated in astrology. In myth, Mercury was the messenger of the gods and transmitted knowledge and information, not only between the gods, but from the gods to men. Astronomically, Mercury is the planet closest to the Sun and symbolically it can be seen as the intermediary between the Sun and all the other planets. Communication is the keyword definition alloted to Mercury, which amounts to anything from the written and spoken word to physical flight! The importance of communication, however, can be understood when one considers that without being able to convey our ideas to anyone, or even more our physical bodies to a particular place, we would lack stimulation, become isolated and mentally atrophied.

Mercury's function in astrology rests in the ability to perceive, to understand and to communicate ideas. In fact it is man's ability to conceptualize that sets him apart from the rest of nature, so in more ways than one Mercury is a gift from the gods. Certainly in synastry, the importance of communication cannot be overestimated, for problems that develop between two people can only be solved providing they communicate with each other.

Mercury is neither a masculine nor a feminine principle; it is abstract and asexual. (This is not to imply, of course, that Geminians are asexual — merely the principle of Mercury itself.) One gets some idea of the quicksilver nature of this planet in strongly Geminian people who can never be pinned down, either mentally or physically, and whose nature is reminiscent of Peter Pan, the eternal child.

Mercury in the Seventh House

People with Mercury in the seventh house usually seek mentally stimulating relationships. Sometimes the partner is a Mercurial type, having this planet (or Gemini and Virgo) emphasized in the chart. Occasionally the partner may be highly strung or even mentally unstable (particularly with afflictions from Uranus or Mercury). Initially the attraction is likely to be towards the partner's mental creativity, the stimulating companionship he or she provides, and the combined exchange of ideas. The individual may be seeking an intellectual as a partner in order to fulfil his or her neglected abilities in this direction. A seventh house Mercury also indicates that the individual may require constant variety and change in his (or her) relationships, so Mercury in this position is not always the best indicator for long-term partnerships.

Perhaps because of the eternal-child quality of this planet, the individual with a seventh house Mercury sometimes has a much younger partner. However, the usual implication of Mercury here applies to the temperamental qualities of the partner, and sometimes to the fact that he or she is involved in journalism or education, for instance, two professions typical of Mercury.

Although the tendency, as we have already seen, is to project the seventh house planet on to the partner, with Mercury in this house the individual has the ability to gain perception not only of other people, but of himself. Thus through his (or her) involvement with others he can encounter many levels of his own being so that much profound insight is accrued.

Venus

In discussing the Sun and Moon, we have seen the fundamental male/female principle at work. In Venus and Mars we have another such pair. In some ways Venus and Mars are more representative of the active drama of the male/female dyad and demonstrate the physical, and especially sexual, energies in a relationship.

Venus in myth was the goddess of beauty and love. In a birth chart, Venus represents the ability to appreciate beauty and our way of creating it; it also represents the way we express affection and form relationships. In a woman's chart, Venus is very much the expression of her femininity and of vital importance in assessing the quality of her experience in relationships. In a man's chart, Venus represents all the aforementioned qualities, yet more often than not these are projected on to the women he seeks. Thus Venus in a man's chart, by sign, house position and aspects, describes the type of woman he is likely to attract to fulfil his own chart potential.

Although the Moon and Venus are both feminine principles, they are subtly different. The Moon has a more spiritual dimension inherent in its nature which Venus does not. In a man's chart, the Moon symbolizes his need to experience the woman on a deep emotional level, whereas Venus represents what he finds immediately attractive about her. In a woman's chart, the Moon is the essence of herself, and Venus the way she plays her womanly role. Perhaps the best way of illustrating this difference is by considering the two Greek words, *agape* and *eros*. The Greeks made a clear division between the two aspects of love. The more spiritual element that exists between father and son or lifelong friends was known as *agape* and originally implied the love between God and man, man and God. Physical love, with its courtship, pleasure and ritual aspects, was known as *eros*, from which we get the word erotic. Not all relationships reflect the Moon *agape* idea, however. The Venus (*eros*) principle is usually first experienced in the attraction between a couple and is then reinforced (or not as the case may be) by a deeper expression of feeling through the Moon (*agape*) nature. It is often in the process of this transition that many relationships flounder.

If Venus is poorly aspected in a birth chart there are likely to be some definite hardships in finding fulfilment and happiness in relationships. In the chart of a woman, difficult aspects to Venus (particularly from Saturn and Uranus) suggest that she may have some considerable difficulty in relating to her feminine role.

Venus in the Seventh House

This is traditionally one of the best placings for Venus. It is in the house that it naturally rules, and is therefore exceedingly strong. People with Venus in the seventh house want their relationships to be beautiful. Great store is set by the appearance of the partnership to the rest of the world — the individual wants himself (or herself) and the partner to be regarded as a perfect couple. However, the individual with this planet in the seventh house may be so concerned with perfection in his or her relationships that small imperfections and incidents become magnified, which can gradually undermine the partnership.

Although a seventh house Venus can indicate a partner who is attractive and gracious in his or her dealings with others, there is no guarantee that the relationship will be plain sailing. A poorly-aspected Venus (particularly by the Moon, Saturn, Uranus, Neptune and Pluto) can indicate frustrations, disappointments and set-backs in relationships, even a partner who is less than an asset to the individual.

Sometimes a person with this position of Venus expects the partner to make the relationship beautiful for him (or her) and forgets his (or her) own contribution to that ideal. In this way, all too often the partner is meant to be the one to apologize or placate the individual. However, a well-aspected Venus goes a long way (providing other chart factors support this) to indicate harmonious and mutually pleasurable relationships.

Mars

Mars, like the Sun, is a masculine principle, yet more representative of man in a strictly physical sense. Ancient Man saw Mars as a fiery planet because of its redness, and in myth he was the god of war. Astrologically, Mars symbolizes creative, dynamic energy. As the counterpart to Venus, which is largely passive, harmony- and beauty-loving, Mars is competitive, challenging and action-seeking. If Venus shows us our ability to create beauty and harmony, Mars shows us our ability to assert ourselves, and seek out our desires and satisfy them. Mars represents physical and sexual energy, and shows how easily and in what manner one's passions are aroused.

Traditionally, a woman's role has been more passive (more Venus oriented) and although Mars may reside in every woman's chart, its dynamic, aggressive nature finds a man a more suitable 'vehicle' for this kind of energy. So Mars in a woman's chart (by sign, house position and aspects) is often more descriptive of the kind of man she is seeking. Mars and the Sun may both be masculine principles, but like the Moon and Venus, they are subtly different. The Sun represents the fundamental nature of a man — his individuality. Mars demonstrates a more physical, externalized expression of himself. If Mars is poorly aspected in a man's chart, he may have difficulty in fitting comfortably into his masculine role (particularly with square and opposition aspects from Saturn and Neptune). Thus the situation of Mars in a man's chart can give the astrologer much information about the way he handles his role in relationships.

Mars in the Seventh House

Mars can present a few problems in the seventh house. The combative nature of Mars in an eminently peace-seeking house brings to mind images of the proverbial bull (or rather ram) in a china shop! The individual with a seventh house Mars is seeking excitement and challenge in his relationships. Sometimes a degree of competitiveness occurs between a couple when the individual has Mars in this position, as he (or she) can feel threatened by the partner's dominance and is liable to retaliate at the slightest provocation.

Conversely, a seventh house Mars can indicate that the individual would rather assert himself through the partner and consequently may often spur the other into action on his behalf. Mars finds peace and harmony basically antithetical to its nature, so individuals with Mars here tend to engineer arguments and explosive situations simply to create a more exciting atmosphere.

Mars in this position can describe the partner as a Martian type (with a strong Mars or Aries well featured in the chart) or the partner may have a Mars-associated career, perhaps in the armed forces or sport.

One of the dangers of a seventh-house Mars is that the potential for competitiveness and argumentative tendencies can develop into open aggression. Individuals with a poorly aspected Mars in this house may be particularly prone to marital violence, and indeed to a certain amount of friction in most relationships.

The individual with Mars in the seventh house needs to recognize his own strength and find his independence, otherwise strife and disharmony can colour his (or her) relationships.

Jupiter

The Sun, Moon, Mercury, Venus and Mars are known as the personal planets for they symbolize personal drives. From Mars onwards we move into the less personal sphere where man is in touch with higher 'energies'.

Jupiter is the largest planet in the solar system. In myth, Jupiter (Zeus in Greek mythology) was King of the Gods and in astrological symbolism Jupiter certainly has a larger than life quality. This planet is also known as the Greater Benefic (Venus being the Lesser) and is considered to exert a tremendously beneficial influence in a chart. The keyword for this planet is expansion, in keeping with Jupiter's philosophical, magnanimous principles; yet this planet can also lead to excess, which is a less pleasant aspect of its nature. But above all, Jupiter represents growth, which can be seen in two ways. Firstly, it can apply to financial increase, to becoming powerful, even famous. Secondly, growth can be applied to learning, to the expansion of consciousness and the love of philosophy and religion.

Although some astrologers take a rather jaundiced view of Jupiter (leaning heavily on its excessive, extravagant tendencies), without this planet's expansive, growth-oriented nature, we may lack the urge to see further than the end of our noses or widen our horizons.

Jupiter contacts between two individuals are tremendously important, regardless of the type of relationship. They show how the couple enjoy each other, for without fun and good feelings a relationship is unlikely to flourish and prosper. One person's Jupiter forming harmonious aspects (or conjunctions) with another's personal planets or angles, can be extremely encouraging to that individual, bringing out the very best in him or her. Even some of the more stressful aspects can bring positive reinforcement to the relationship, although negative tendencies can be exaggerated as well.

Jupiter in the Seventh House

As with Venus in the seventh house, Jupiter is a promising sign for successful relationships. The expansive nature of Jupiter can work well on many levels of a partnership. Sometimes an individual with Jupiter here has an exceedingly wealthy and important partner.

Sometimes the partner is generous, honourable and philosophical and sometimes all of these things. Yet with a poorly aspected Jupiter, the less desirable qualities of this planet may be presented in relationships. Thus the individual may find he (or she) is involved with unreliable, extravagant individuals. Occasionally a seventh house Jupiter can indicate a partner who has a strong dominating personality and one who is prone to making exceptionally cruel remarks when angry.

As we have seen with other planets in a seventh house context, although the qualities of a particular planet belong to the individual, more often than not they tend to be projected on to others. With Jupiter he (or she) is drawn to relationships with people who personify wisdom, faith and largesse. In some ways, rather like a person with a seventh house Sun, he (or she) can feel overshadowed by the partner and needs to find his (or her) own Jupiterian qualities.

The attainment of personal and joint growth, wisdom and understanding through relationships is the most important dimension of a Jupiter-tenanted seventh house.

Saturn

Saturn is the next planet on from Jupiter and represents almost exactly the opposite principles. These two, like the Sun and the Moon, Venus and Mars are a planetary pair.

Saturn has been known traditionally as the Greater Malefic (Mars being the Lesser) and as its name implies, Saturn is by no means all sweetness and light. However, Saturn's implication in astrological terms has changed considerably over the past decade. Indeed in 1981 the Voyager II Spacecraft gave us here on Earth our first close-up view of this beautiful planet. Its curious rings made up of thousands of tiny particles and hundreds of bands have deepened its mystery and, symbolically, perhaps we can see that this planet has a richness of meaning yet to be unfolded by astrologers. Far from the mortal dread that earlier astrologers used to show towards Saturn, modern astrologers tend to view this planet as the key to self-discovery, the bridge between one level of consciousness and another.

Saturn in a birth chart needs close and careful consideration. Its keyword principles of limitation and frustration, so familiar to the student, are almost meaningless until they are viewed as part of Saturn's highly complex nature. In myth, Cronos (Saturn) was the god who set the fates in motion, and after castrating his father Ouranus (Uranus) he was left alone to reign over the world in process of formation. It is difficult to comprehend the meaning of Saturn in a birth chart without considering the idea of fate and karma. The blocks and difficulties we experience in life are more often than not related to the position and aspects of Saturn in the natal chart. If we adopt the idea that part of the meaning and purpose of our lives is to come to terms with our actions (past and present) in order to develop into more conscious individuals, then we must encounter Saturn and all he represents in order to do so.

Crystallization, structure and self-discipline are also keyword descriptions of Saturn. These are essential qualities to achieve growth but in a different way from the outpouring, expansive action of Jupiter. Too much self-discipline, too strict an adherence to old patterns of life, however, can lead to rigidity, intolerance and isolation.

Saturn in a chart represents not only what we find difficult and effort-making, but what we fear most will undermine us. In this sense, Saturn has been identified with Jung's 'shadow' — the things we repress because they do not fit in with our self-image (if unrecognized) emerge in their most negative way and become ripe for projection on to others. In a child's mind the night-time hours conjure up fantastic images of monsters and ghouls which suddenly disappear with the switching on of a light. Such a parallel can be drawn with Saturn in a chart: to be conscious of the qualities that Saturn represents, to understand rather than ignore them (or transfer them on to others), is the action of a light in a darkened room. Thus, instead of manifesting the frustration aspect of itself, Saturn can become the teacher and enlighten the individual about the mysteries of his own inner nature.

Saturn contacts between a couple are essential if a relationship is to have any durability and meaning. In fact marriage itself is a highly Saturnine institution, recognized in law, reflecting the couple's responsibility to each other as well as forming a fundamental unit of the structure of society. Thus, although difficult Saturn aspects may indicate frustration and blocks between a couple, the difficulties can also forge much growth and understanding. If both people are open and honest with themselves and each other, Saturn can unite through understanding rather than alienate through resentment, coldness and distance.

Saturn in the Seventh House

The placing of Saturn in the seventh house is never easy, which does not mean that it cannot be successful or rewarding. As we have seen in the description of this planet, Saturn represents the lessons that have to be learned in order to develop into more conscious individuals. So with Saturn in the seventh house, the lessons are found in the experience of one-to-one relationships. The last things one wants to be aware of in connection with love and romance are duty, responsibility, limitations and frustrations. Yet if a partnership is going to stand the test of forty years or so, the presence of a well-aspected Saturn in the seventh house is a considerable help.

As was mentioned in the Introduction, it is through our interaction with others that we begin to see ourselves, and as the 'action' of Saturn is to make us aware of our whole nature (the darker, more hidden aspects particularly), with Saturn 'exalted' in this house, we have the greatest opportunity to do so.

However, this growth is not achieved without overcoming some hurdles in relationships. Saturn in the seventh can indicate the attraction of the individual to an older partner or father-figure (as we have seen in the case of Eva Braun), and although it is rather difficult to see 'father' represented by a woman in a man's seventh house, Saturn here frequently indicates the attraction to very efficient, highly disciplined, 'mature' women. Sometimes the partner becomes a burden to the individual (either through weakness or constraint) but this is unlikely to emerge until well into the relationship. Saturn can also indicate the partner has a Capricorn emphasis or a strong Saturn in his (or her) own natal chart.

A seventh house Saturn shows that the individual is seeking security in a relationship (perhaps even 'playing-safe') and the more evidence of this security in a material sense, the better. However, the urge for the latter in marriage is often at the expense of a true emotional rapport, and the crystallizing aspect of Saturn can be seen in the way the structure of the marriage assumes a prison-like quality for the individual.

Sometimes the individual experiences not only loneliness in the marriage through the lack of any emotional bond, but also physical separation, even cruelty and unfaithfulness. Sometimes Saturn here signifies that the individual is likely to marry late, or possibly not at all. But this is not *always* the case. As Saturn represents that which we must come to terms with, in order to make us whole, the experience is appropriate to the individual. The one assured factor with a seventh house Saturn is that the relationships encountered are never light-hearted.

In keeping with the Saturn cycle,[2] many of the inherent lessons of a seventh house Saturn are experienced up to and around the twenty-ninth year of life. At this point many issues centering on relationships can be resolved, provided the individual becomes aware of his own contribution to them. According to the amount of insight gained, the experiences do not necessarily have to repeat themselves. In view of coming to terms with our actions (past and present) Saturn can symbolize a particular karmic link with the partner that involves some service or sacrifice on the individual's behalf.

Saturn in the seventh house, even if it has splendid aspects, still involves the individual in some learning experience through relationships. In her book *Saturn*, Liz Greene suggests that the individual with a seventh house Saturn is seeking inner integration and that his (or her) intimate encounters with others are 'involved in the working out of the process of inner discovery'. In this way Saturn indicates two themes in this position: that 'the marriage partner can become a source of suffering or a source of great opportunity for individual growth'.

Uranus

Up until the end of the eighteenth century, Saturn was considered to be the outermost planet in the solar system. With the discovery of Uranus in 1781, man's sense of (astronomic) proportion changed radically, synchronizing with the revolutionary tone of the times. Astrologically, Uranus represents change, upheaval, the awakening of higher consciousness and the development of intuitive and spiritual faculties. As with the other trans-Saturnian planets, its theme is on a collective level rather than personal, influencing generations rather than individuals, unless strongly placed in the birth chart.

In myth, Uranus, King of Heaven, was castrated and dethroned by his son Cronos (Saturn). He was a tyrannical king and kept his earthly children (the Titans) deep in the earth, where they were unable to see the light. A parallel can be drawn here with the awakening of higher consciousness that Uranus represents. This would be too powerful to be unleashed indiscriminately on man — he would be blinded by its impact. So man remains in material darkness until, guided by Saturn, he has developed to the point where he can appreciate the mysteries of heaven.

[2] The passage of Saturn through the Zodiac which takes, on average, twenty-nine years.

Uranus becomes a more personal idea in a birth chart through its house position and aspects to the personal planets. A strongly Uranian person needs unrestrained freedom of self-expression — hence its esoteric association as the higher octave of the Sun. Uranian individuals dislike being dominated by others or adhering to routine or convention, so on the one hand there are Uranian types who are inventive geniuses but also those who are 'rebels without a cause'.

Uranian energies between a couple can indicate sudden, magnetic attraction, but unless both are prepared to allow each other plenty of freedom this energy can be rather selfish and destructive in long-term partnerships.

Uranus in the Seventh House

All the outer planets are difficult 'energies' to handle and express in a seventh house position. Uranus, representing unrestrained freedom and unpredictability, does not adapt too well to the the conventional structure of marriage, or indeed to any long-term partnership. Individuals with Uranus in the seventh house find their relationships difficult to keep on an even keel; breaks and separations occur all too easily. Sometimes the individual is attracted to unconventional, bohemian types who subsequently play havoc with his (or her) life. Again we see the element of projection here in that the individual is attracted to unusual, iconoclastic partners, since this need goes unrecognized in his own nature. Uranus here can also indicate that the partner is an Aquarian or a strongly Uranian type.

Uranus, like Saturn, appears in many guises in the seventh house. Traditionally, this placing has been identified with a certain propensity towards divorce, and although many individuals with Uranus in the seventh house do experience this kind of trauma, it is not *always* so. Uranus in the seventh house indicates a desire for change and to experience the unusual (usually at high-voltage), which may mean that the individual (or the partner) seeks extra stimulation outside the confines of marriage. (Peter Sellars, Elizabeth Taylor, Yoko Ono and Margaret Trudeau, wife of the Canadian Prime-Minister, all have Uranus in the seventh!) Frequently in my own work I find individuals with a Uranus-tenanted seventh house running into difficulties with long-term partnerships. It seems that in keeping with the myth of Uranus and the Titans, until the individual has developed enough self-awareness, the high-frequency energy of Uranus tends to work on its most disturbing level, causing much tension and unpredictability in relationships.

There is another side to Uranus, however, that offers the individual the possibility of considerable growth through one-to-one encounters. Harmonious aspects to Uranus are helpful in providing the individual with an easier path to the attainment of such Uranian principles as equality and freedom of self-expression. But the stressful aspects (particularly from the Sun, Moon, Venus and Mars) can be upseting, even chaotic for the individual to handle. Sometimes the individual seeks out a partner who will share his (or her) experimental 'free-love' approach to relationships. Sometimes there is a vast age difference or the partner may come from a distant country (or even a different social group). He (or she) may have been married before or have an unusual background. In a sense this reflects the individual's own revolution within his psyche, and in choosing a partner that flouts convention, he can vicariously break out of the rigidity and structure of his life.

Occasionally a seventh house Uranus is indicative of one partner out-growing the other so that there is no way the relationship can be maintained in its existing form. Thus the relationship may be broken rather abruptly, leaving behind much bitterness and resentment.

On the positive side, a Uranus-tenanted seventh house can indicate the possibility of an unusual relationship, in which both partners experience a unique rapport and where ultimately their shared experience stimulates mutual growth and awareness.

Neptune

Beyond Uranus, we find Neptune. Like the Sun and Moon, Venus and Mars, and Jupiter and Saturn before them, Uranus and Neptune are a male/female dyad — Uranus representing the male principle and Neptune, the female. Neptune is the second of the transpersonal planets and its discovery in 1846 synchronized with the great romantic movement and the advent of hypnotism and Spiritualism. Although in myth Neptune was a male deity, he actually embodied female principles. Astrologically, Neptune is considered to be the higher octave of the Moon (and in some teachings, Venus), both of which are feminine principles.

Neptune in a birth chart symbolizes man's ability to transcend earthly limitations. In this way Neptune becomes the artist's muse, the poet's inspiration and the mystic's inner vision. However, as with Uranus, these higher vibrations are difficult for man to incorporate into everyday life and all too often the more negative properties of this planet are encountered. Thus Neptune's urge to escape or transcend physical reality may manifest in the abuse of drugs or alcohol, or a tendency to deceive and create chaos and confusion. Neptune has close associations with the world of film and photography. The concept of images on celluloid reflects Neptune's ephemeral nature; its images can be perceived and impressions absorbed in such a way that the senses and the imagination are highly stimulated. Neptunian 'vibrations' are the most subtle and elusive of the planets. There is a fine line between reality and illusion, enlightenment and self-delusion, and most people find the heightened experience of Neptune difficult to sustain.

Neptunian 'energies' are often encountered in the early stages of a relationship in the romantic haze that surrounds the love-object, the feeling of floating on air and the loss of appetite and concentration. In due course, however, perception assumes its normal, everyday state and a sense of ennui may ensue.

Neptune contacts between a couple show, on the one hand, the level of empathy and compassion shared with each other and, on the other, the level of deceit and disappointment working to undermine the relationship. But with care and control, Neptune can lead the individual into heightened states of perception and true spiritual experience and vision.

Neptune in the Seventh House

A Neptune-tenanted seventh house can be the source of some considerable difficulty and confusion in relationships. The individual with Neptune here is looking for an ideal relationship that provides emotional and physical fulfilment and, most important of all, a kind of spiritual soul union. The element of projection in this case is second to none. The individual is often swept off his feet by someone, placing him (or her) on a pedestal, only to find some time later that the prince(ss) was a frog after all.

The martyr/saviour complex is often present too. The individual may be drawn to partners in order to 'save' them or help them fulfil their potential, thus sacrificing his (or her) own needs for the partner's. Sometimes the partner becomes completely dependent on the individual, perhaps because he is a weak character or chronically ill, maybe even an alcoholic. In this way the individual 'martyrs' himself (or herself) for the relationship.

As in the case of Saturn in this position, the difficulties of Neptune do not emerge at the beginning of a relationship. Usually the individual is quite blind at first to the other person's faults because the projection is so strong. When, in time, the real person starts to emerge, the individual feels let down, even betrayed by the partner: 'I can't imagine what I saw in him' or 'How could she change so much?' are all too familiar cries from the individual with a Neptune-tenanted seventh house.

Sometimes, of course, the individual *is* badly let down in a relationship, for Neptune in this position can indicate the tendency to be attracted to unreliable partners who subsequently cause the individual much pain and unhappiness. Occasionally the partner leaves the relationship for no apparent reason or claims that he (or she) has never really been happy and has many previously unspoken feelings of animosity towards the individual. The quality of deception is always a possibility with Neptune in this house. Sometimes facts about the partner's background emerge after a long-term commitment has been made, leaving the individual shattered emotionally. Sometimes, of course, the partner may have Pisces well represented in the chart or a strong Neptune.

The process of inner discovery and psycho-spiritual growth is represented in the most challenging and rewarding way by Saturn, Uranus, Neptune and Pluto in this house. Although the negative properties of Neptune are often evident in relationships, this is perhaps because the true experience offered here is not on the physical plane. The union sought by Neptune in the seventh is a mystical one. Thus Neptune at its best offers a person the opportunity of finding a true soul mate with whom there is a mutual sense of belonging and empathy on all levels. In the main, however, there is a tendency to place unrealistic goals on relationships and seek a perfection that rarely exists in reality. In a sense, the individual's unconscious yearning to reach a higher plane is felt to be provided through the partner and if this does not happen he (or she) feels disappointed and let down.

Pluto

Pluto is the outermost known planet in the solar system. Its discovery in 1930 synchronized with the splitting of the atom, the Wall Street Crash and the rise of depth psychology. In myth, Pluto was the god of the underworld and although a fearful, rapacious deity, his kingdom contained vast riches and treasure. An astrological parallel can be drawn in that although the situations encountered through Pluto seem overpowering and traumatic, they reveal great truths and insight that enrich the individual on a psychic level. Astrologically, Pluto symbolizes death and rebirth, elimination and transformation. Its aspects to the personal planets in the birth chart enable the individual to find his inner source of power and bring about evolutionary changes in his own psyche. Thus the unconscious becomes conscious through profound, purging and sometimes cathartic experiences.

The three outer planets symbolize man's connection with higher, more subtle levels of experience and each planet presents these archetypal themes in a different way. Uranus challenges man to discard outworn structures of thought and to revolutionize his ideas through attunement to a higher source. Neptune seeks to lift man's spirit into the realms of pure transcendent experience — at-one-ness with God. Pluto urges man to bring about changes deep in his consciousness, and thus transform his life.

Pluto is a subtle, yet powerful symbol in the horoscope. An individual who has Pluto well featured in the birth chart may have a strong sense of destiny, but this planet's influence can be either strongly constructive or destructive, producing Plutonian people of great spiritual calibre or those who become arch-criminals. In some esoteric teachings Pluto is considered to be the higher octave of Mercury,[3] which can be seen in their common quest for knowledge. With Mercury, this is based on intellectual enquiry, whereas with Pluto the quest is for secret, hidden knowledge involving inner journeys of the psyche.

Pluto contacts in a relationship are powerful and transforming or violent and destructive, according to the level of awareness of the two individuals concerned. The nature of Pluto is often compulsive and obsessive and this is reflected in the intensity of the contact between a couple. The difficult aspects involving Pluto can indicate power struggles and ego-conflicts but, as with the more harmonious aspects, there is also a transforming quality about them.

Pluto in the Seventh House

An individual with Pluto in his (or her) seventh house is unlikely to seek superficial relationships, yet there may be considerable difficulty in establishing a satisfactory and close rapport with

[3] In myth, Hermes (Mercury) conveyed the souls of the dead to Hades (Pluto's kingdom).

The link between the Mercury-ruled sign, Gemini (the Heavenly Twins), is outlined in Joan Hodgson's book *The Sacred Science*. The division of life between the earth and the heavens, illustrated by the immortal Pollux and his mortal twin Castor, is paralleled by the same light and dark aspects of Pluto.

Mercury's Caduceus, with its symmetrical, bilateral arrangement of two snakes (representing wisdom) on a staff (representing power), is, as J. E. Circlot points out in his *Dictionary of Symbols*, symbolic of 'opposing forces balancing one another in such a way to create a higher static form'.

others. The individual is often drawn to powerful and demanding partners who manipulate and control him (or her) albeit by subtle manoeuvres. There is a somewhat fated quality about the individual's relationships and the involvement is usually intense and highly complex. The partner may be a Plutonic type having a strong Scorpio or Pluto emphasis in his (or her) chart. This position may also describe the partner as a deep-thinking, penetrating individual.

As we have seen with Saturn, Uranus and Neptune, these 'heavy' planets in the seventh house have a powerful effect on the individual on an inner level. As Pluto represents regeneration and elimination, its effect can be seen as the shedding of an old skin to reveal another; the old giving birth to the revivified. When Pluto is in the seventh house the individual is using his relationships to unfold this process. Thus, the partner becomes the catalyst for the individual's evolutionary changes in his (or her) psyche. Unfortunately, the individual is often entirely unaware of this process, feeling only the powerful experience of the relationship itself.

With Pluto in this position the individual is often experiencing the working-out of a karmic relationship — hence the compulsive attraction and sense of destiny accompanying the partnership. In this way many of the conflicts and powerful exchanges that arise between a couple are exceedingly deep-rooted and difficult to sort out rationally or objectively. However, the opportunity being offered is to do precisely that — to cleanse the psyche through the intensity of a powerful relationship.

Certainly the effects of Pluto in this position can be traumatic and relationships frequently lurch from crisis to crisis. Jealousies, possessiveness and emotional games are usually present with this placing. Sometimes an element of mistrust, even fear, develops between the individual and the partner and a certain amount of suppression and control is felt through the partnership. Occasionally, cruelty, both physical and mental, occurs within relationships too. In effect it is the individual's own need to break through restrictions in his (or her) own nature that causes him (or her) to feel the partner is to blame for the difficulties. Sometimes the partner cuts off emotionally for fear of encountering deeper feelings, or alternatively it is the individual himself (or herself) who blocks this response in the partner.

Although much has been said about the difficulties, a Pluto-tenanted seventh house can also indicate relationships of considerable depth, passion and longevity. The total commitment and security needed in relationships can only be found, however, through personal changes brought about by the individual's awareness of his inner nature. The partner and the partnership work to bring about this process so that the relationship provides a source of transformation for both people.

In all the preceeding descriptions of the planets in the seventh house, the same factors apply in a lesser extent to the sign on the cusp of this house when no actual planet is present. Thus, if Libra is on the Descendant, the qualities of a Venus-tenanted seventh house will be relevant, but judged according to the sign, aspects and placing of Venus.

Complications can also arise if there is more than one planet to consider in this house. Each planet must then be judged on its own merit and a synthesis made combining all the factors. Some astrologers maintain that each planet represents a definitive relationship, but in my own work I have not really found this to be true. Planets in the seventh house represent the factors needed to make the individual 'whole' and if more than one symbol is there, the individual may find all these factors personified in one major relationship (or marriage) or that two or three relationships are needed. It must also be remembered that the seventh house covers *all* one-to-one relationships, and most people have more than one intimate encounter during their lifetime. Thus the symbolism inherent in this house provides the background colour to all relationships of this kind. In this way one person can bring out the best potential of an individual's seventh house and another, the worst. Once a natal chart has been thoroughly explored, taking into consideration all the planets and indications of the seventh house, the astrologer has a sound basis on which to assess the comparison of one horoscope and another.

4.
CASE STUDIES (II)

Sing and dance together and be joyous
but let each of you be alone
even as the strings of a lute are alone
though they quiver to the same music.

Kahlil Gibran

'Character is destiny' is often quoted in reference to astrology to demonstrate that the individual carries within him the seeds of potential to be a resounding success or a dismal failure. The horoscope is a map of destiny in this sense — a blue-print of potential. The individual's capacity to use his abilities wisely and well is the key to his eventual 'destination'.

For some individuals life seems to get off to a bad start from which they never really recover, whereas others seem to be fortunate from the very beginning and experience happiness and success in most aspects of their lives. In other cases a bad start can often generate a determination in the individual to alter his course, through his own will. In astrology the charts with the most difficult configurations frequently 'produce' extremely fine individuals, which illustrates that self-knowledge and growth is almost always achieved through painful experience. Just why some individuals have more than their share of these difficulties can be seen in karmic terms or in psychological ones — that the individual attracts into his life the experiences that reflect his inner state. Once the inner man is well, the outer life will show harmony.

The chart shown in Figure 10 is that of a woman who has had many difficult experiences in her life, the most poignant of which have been encountered in relationships. Elaine was the second and last child of middle-class English parents. Her father was an engineer in the Royal Navy and frequently absent from home (in fact she saw her father for the first time when she was three). There was one brother, eight years older than herself, with whom she has always had an unsatisfactory relationship.

The problems began early in life, largely in the form of a difficult mother-daughter relationship. Her mother (a Sun Taurus) pre-

Figure 10: Elaine's chart.

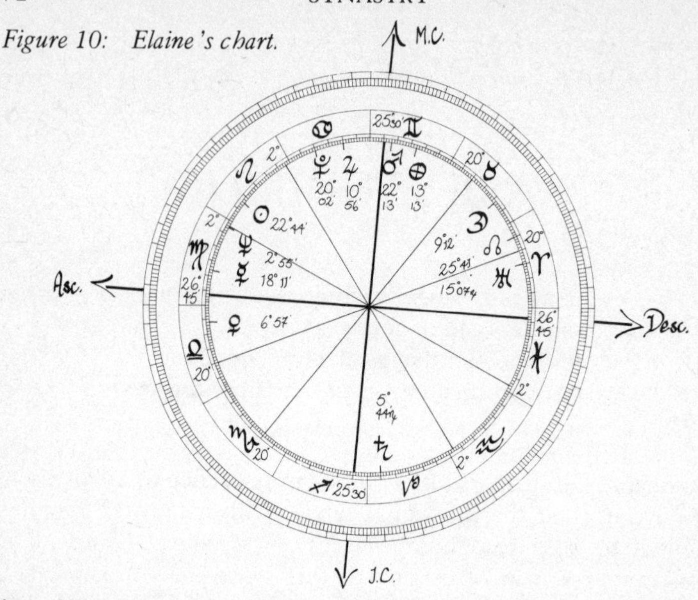

ferred boys and most of her energy and maternal support was given to her son. Elaine was unfortunate to have been born at a time when the general view was that women had to be domesticated before being educated, and so it was her brother who was given the encouragement and academic opportunities. Elaine's mother was exceedingly critical of her (despite her intelligence and attractiveness) and although there was no serious violence, her mother's attacks were both verbally and physically vicious. Fortunately, Elaine and her father had a warm, loving relationship (although somewhat sporadic), which compensated for the lack of any real love or understanding from her mother. Elaine had the message firmly implanted from an early age that boys (particularly her brother) were on the winning side whilst girls (particularly herself) were lesser mortals. Consequently, Elaine adopted a rebellious and belligerent attitude to almost everything; she became a 'tom-boy', enjoying the company of boys and competing with them.

Elaine had few close friends during her childhood and adolescence, and although she mixed with the boys she never had a boyfriend as such. At the age of seventeen she experienced an attempted rape, but managed to fight off her attacker. The same evening she had a tumultuous row with her mother, after which she left home and took the ferry to the Channel Islands. Up until this time Elaine had been working as an apprentice hairdresser, but once in the Channel Islands she successfully applied for the position of manageress in a beauty parlour.

After leaving home and the everyday influence of her mother Elaine's life began to improve. She found a surrogate mother in the form of her landlady, who understood and emotionally supported her. Three years later at the age of twenty she met her first husband, Emil. On meeting him she experienced all the sensations of love at first sight, yet refused bluntly to go out with him for six months. Elaine feels in retrospect that this was not only because Emil posed a threat to her independence but that she sensed he held some difficulty for her. This was certainly true. None of Emil's family attended the wedding and on the few occasions she met his mother, intense animosity was displayed towards her.

Emil was Elaine's first love in every sense of the phrase, and as a sexual novice, she felt the physical side of their relationship was perfect. During the last night of the honeymoon, however, she was a little miffed when Emil spent most of the evening engrossed in conversation with another man, eventually suggesting she went back to the hotel alone. He returned at 5.30 the following morning. During the course of the next few months Elaine realized that there was something 'not quite right' with the physical side of their marriage. Emil made sexual demands on her with which she felt loath to comply. Within nine months of the marriage she discovered that he was a homosexual. The trauma of this revelation combined with her deep love of Emil propelled her into a physical and mental breakdown. Two or three attempts were made at a reconciliation but the final break came on Elaine's discovery of a letter between Emil and his mother revealing an incestuous family relationship. Divorce was granted some five years later, but it took seventeen years for Elaine to come to terms with losing Emil.

Despite her emotional traumas, Elaine was exceedingly successful in her business and enjoyed both her power and independence. Two years after her divorce from Emil, Elaine met her second husband Anthony, who was himself already married at that time. Despite her coolness towards him, Anthony pursued her with great zest, ultimately leaving his wife. Elaine and Anthony married two years later, having already produced one son. Although Anthony was extremely loving and generous towards her, Elaine was unhappy within the marriage. The reason was that she felt no real love for Anthony — a factor not helped by her inability to resolve her feelings for Emil. Three years into their marriage, Anthony's career took them to live in the West Indies — ironically a few hundred miles from where Emil was by then living. Knowing her feelings for Emil, Anthony arranged for her to fly over and visit Emil as a Christmas present. The day before she left, Emil was killed in a car crash.

Elaine's marriage to Anthony gradually deteriorated. Anthony, already a heavy drinker before his marriage, turned to drugs as well, from which he eventually died four years later.

Elaine returned to England on Anthony's death and set up a new business simultaneously bringing up two young sons single-handed. Problems soon developed between the two boys. The elder, well-balanced and academically very bright, gained a scholarship to an excellent school, whilst the younger seemed set on under-achieving, sought the company of the local 'toughs' and got into trouble with the police. Both boys disliked each other intensely and their continual sparring made family life intolerable. This combined with the pressure of running a business brought Elaine to financial and emotional collapse more than once. Six years after Anthony's death, she attempted suicide. At no time did Elaine receive any support (moral or otherwise) from her mother and brother (her father had died when she was twenty-seven), which duly increased her sense of isolation. She continued to immerse herself in the business, coping as well as she could with both boys now approaching adolescence. She avoided close relationships and at times cut off her feelings from everyone.

This state of affairs continued for four years until she met the third man in her life, Luke. Luke was unhappily married, to a dominant and unsympathetic wife, and although both he and Elaine made a determined effort not to get involved, their mutually strong feelings precipitated them into a love affair. This time Elaine felt the happiest she had ever been in her life. She and Luke were physically and temperamentally suited; he supported her through her business difficulties and, with his attentions, the younger son began to find a new direction. Within a year of the affair Luke's company promoted him to a top position in their Kenyan branch. He 'had no alternative but to accept' and in consequence the relationship was severed. A few months later, Elaine's health broke down, resulting in hospitalization.

Climbing slowly back to health, Elaine began to assess her life to see where and how she could change the general pattern of hurt and disappointment. A chronic and inoperable spinal condition (which began when she was seventeen) had caused her considerable pain for many years — a condition made worse by each successive pregnancy. During her stay in hospital a blind physiotherapist began to treat her. She not only relieved much of the pain through massage, but encouraged Elaine to try autogenic treatment. These two factors began to release the stress that had built up over the years in physical, emotional and mental terms. Psychic changes occurred too, accompanied by a desire for a new spiritual dimension in her life. Also during this time, Alan, a profoundly spiritual man she had known for a year, began to play an increasingly important role in her life. Their relationship was close and mutually empathetic. With Alan's encouragement, Elaine began to feel an inner strength and conviction to allow this new (spiritual) dimension to operate in her life.

During the past six months Elaine has been going through a slow process of self-discovery. She feels that one of her main sources of difficulty is an almost pathological need to be in control all the time. She grew up feeling she had a fight on her hands and her life has become a sort of independent struggle against the odds. In order to control every aspect of her life, she needed to be able to detach herself from the feelings that made her vulnerable and easily manipulated. This she had learned from childhood. Consequently, although she yearned for happiness and love, she unconsciously blocked any relationship that involved sharing her true self through her fear of being hurt. Three of the partners she chose all denied her the opportunity of a true marriage and indeed presented her with situations patently beyond her control.

Astrologically, Elaine's chart portrays a vivid and accurate picture of her complex nature and problematic life. The chart, although dominated by a difficult 'Grand Cross' in cardinal signs does not lack redeeming features. The Sun in Leo is in its own sign; the Moon is exalted in Taurus and both luminaries are well aspected. The major source of difficulty in Elaine's chart is a problematic Saturn forming the 'handle' of a 'bucket-type' shaping. Saturn, despite being dignified in its own sign of Capricorn is made considerably more of a burden by its placing in the fourth house. The I.C. and the fourth house represent home; one's origins and one's roots — psychologically, emotionally and literally. Saturn's presence in this sensitive house exerts an austere and unremitting influence. From her earliest childhood Elaine felt unloved; she was the archetypal black sheep of the family. Saturn in the fourth house frequently shows unhappiness in childhood and an over-emphasis on discipline and duty. It can also depict the absence of one parent (particularly father), which was aptly illustrated by the intermittent appearance of Elaine's sea-going father. As a sensitive little girl, Elaine subconsciously formed the opinion that as the one person through whom she experienced love also hurt her by constantly disappearing, men were not be relied upon. Saturn also squares the Ascendant and from a fourth position reinforces the home difficulties which helped undermine her self-esteem.

Although the Moon is exalted in Taurus — a sign embodying emotional stability — this essentially feminine symbol is in aspect to Saturn. The Moon/Saturn link shows that Elaine is deeply sensitive but that the feelings are controlled, even crushed by Saturn's constraining qualities. The Moon, also representative of mother, admirably demonstrates the lack of emotional response and unaffectionate nature of Elaine's mother. Certainly it could be argued that the trine aspect *must* indicate harmony between these two ideas. But as we know just how damaging Elaine's early experience of her mother was in regard to her ability to express her feelings confidently and openly, the inherent lack of sympathy between Moon and Saturn is clearly shown. Jupiter and Pluto placed in the tenth house (the former involved in the Grand Cross) also throw some light on the parental situation. As her mother was the more influential factor here, she emerges as both Jupiter and Pluto — an all-powerful, manipulative figure.

Emotions that cannot find a free and happy outlet for expression all too often manifest as physical problems. In Elaine's case, the backbone (an integral part of the skeleton, ruled by Saturn) took the stress of her emotional pain. It is highly significant that at the age of seventeen, when she experienced an attempted rape and finally left home, the spinal problems began. (This coincided with a transiting Saturn/Pluto conjunction that squared her Moon, thereby bringing the natal Moon/Saturn conflict into focus; Saturn later that year conjoined her radical Sun whilst transiting Uranus crossed to and fro over the Midheaven. Progressed Moon conjoined natal Saturn in the month of the crisis.)

Saturn causes further problems for Elaine by forming a close square aspect to her Venus, yet another feminine symbol. This aspect is also co-incident with unhappy childhood experiences. As Venus represents the ability to form relationships and to express and receive affection — in fact to find happiness — Saturn also places a restriction here. This aspect appears with unfailing regularity in the charts of women who feel insecure about their appearance and their ability to attract men who will love them for themselves. Paradoxically, these women are frequently exceedingly attractive, yet have an aura of untouchability and aloofness about them. Almost as an antidote to the feelings of inadequacy accompanying Moon and Venus/Saturn aspects, a woman will endeavour to succeed out in the world. Elaine's one compensation for her relationship difficulties has been her ability in the business sphere. (Of course Sun in Leo, sextile Mars conjunct the Midheaven also pin-points the career drive and will to succeed.)

Rejection is a theme usually present in the lives of those with Venus/Saturn contacts and the square aspect is perhaps the most difficult to contend with. Elaine was actively rejected by Emil and Luke and with her second husband, Anthony, the situation was reversed (which was just as distressing).

Elaine's seventh house gives a graphic description of her relationships with Emil, Anthony, Luke and Alan. With Pisces on the cusp of the Descendant, Neptune, the ruler in the twelfth house is shown as a strong factor in three of her relationships. Emil (with whom she was deeply in love) was a homosexual, and indeed many disturbing factors about his life emerged late in their marriage. (He, incidentally, was a Sun Gemini, reflecting Elaine's Mars in that sign on the Midheaven.) All the hopes and expectations projected on to Emil and the marriage crumbled into dust with the discovery of his homosexuality. His inability to have a normal physical relationship increased her sense of failure as a woman and reinforced the rejection theme. (Elaine's progressed Venus had reached a conjunction to her South node in the year she met Emil, and by the time they separated, her progressed Mars was opposing her natal Saturn.)

Anthony was an alcoholic, ultimately dying from drink and drugs; both activities are highly Neptunian. This, too, was a marriage full of disappointments and unrequited love. (Anthony's Sun was placed at 10° of Capricorn and thus formed a conjunction with Elaine's Saturn opposing Jupiter and squaring Venus and Uranus, thereby triggering her Grand Cross. Elaine met Anthony when she was twenty-nine — the year of her Saturn Return.)

Alan is the third Neptunian figure in her life. This time Neptune, 'the mystic' emerges as a theme. Alan is deeply committed to spiritual matters. He and Elaine have an intuitive understanding and empathy with each other, yet at this stage, the relationship remains platonic. (Alan is a Sun Virgo; his Neptune is conjunct Elaine's Ascendant; her Neptune is conjunct his Mercury whilst his Neptune is conjunct her's. Their relationship blossomed whilst Neptune formed a conjunction to Elaine's I.C.)

The Neptunian content to her relationships can also be seen in the formation of a Grand Trine involving the Moon, Saturn and Neptune, all of which are placed in the three water houses. There are extremely sensitive, compassionate and psychic properties in this formation as well as the elements of sacrifice, suffering and pain.

Luke is the only partner not entirely reflecting the Neptunian influence of her seventh house. Luke is a strongly Arian personality, again reflecting Elaine's dominant Mars. He also has a Leo Ascendant forming a conjunction to Elaine's Sun. Thus his Descendant is ruled by Uranus, the same planet to be found in Elaine's seventh house. Uranus embodies the principle of freedom and in the seventh house indicates the attraction of the unusual and unattainable. Luke, of course, was married and in the final analysis unable to leave his wife. Elaine felt the happiest and most able to be herself during her relationship with Luke. His Mars/Uranus conjunction was exactly conjunct her Moon in Taurus; the separation occurred on an eclipse squaring transiting Uranus. There is, however, still the suspicion of a Neptunian influence with Luke, for Neptune in his natal chart forms the handle to his bucket-shaping, which coincidentally conjoins Elaine's natal Mercury.

What is of course so pertinent from an astrological point of view is not only that Elaine's experience of relationships distinctly reflects the Neptune/Uranus influence in the seventh house and her chart's overall strong Saturn content, but that the partners themselves have the relevant astrological factors strongly featured in their own charts. Furthermore, their influence in her life occurs at a time when the planets in question are much in evidence (by progression and transit).

Although Elaine's well-aspected Sun and Moon/Jupiter sextile do much to relieve the stresses and strains of the Grand Cross, this configuration is fundamental to her relationship difficulties. Poor Venus, strong in its own sign, ruler of the second house of feelings — and rising to boot — is the one personal planet caught up in this configuration. Thus the over-indulgence and excess of the Venus/Jupiter square, the emotional instability and wilfulness of the Uranus/Venus opposition and the blocking action of Saturn are locked in a vicious circle, perpetually at the mercy of any transit or progression to its four points.

Many people born in Elaine's year have a similar configuration. Perhaps the most notable is Princess Margaret, whose birthday falls one week after Elaine's. Princess Margaret's chart is given in Figure 11 and shows the Grand Cross in a reversed position. In this case Saturn and Venus are not only in their own signs but in their own houses *and* angular; Jupiter (exalted in Cancer) and Uranus are also widely conjunct the I.C. and Ascendant points respectively. Princess Margaret has had a similarly traumatic time with her relationships, involving considerable pain, rejection and disillusion. She relinquished her first love, Peter Townsend, for 'duty to her family and her country', as the relationship threatened to bring

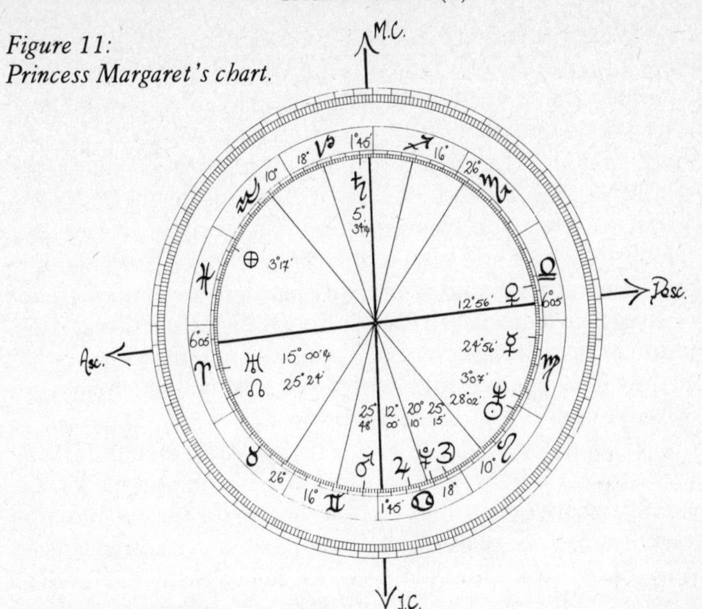

Figure 11: Princess Margaret's chart.

down the government of the time. Her relationship with Anthony Armstrong-Jones, described as a 'fairy-tale romance', developed into open hostility, independent lives, and ultimate divorce. (Margaret has a Sun/Neptune conjunction which Tony Armstong-Jones reflected as a Sun/Pisces, with Mars in his twelfth house and Neptune exactly conjunct his Descendant.) The initial attraction for Tony was his bohemian life-style and his non-conformity to aristocratic or indeed royal form.

Princess Margaret, sometimes referred to as 'the rebel Princess', has become a highly controversial member of the Royal Family. She is creative, talented and charismatic; encouraged as a child to dance and do as she pleased, in adulthood she has been denied any outlet for her creativity. Uranus rising shows an almost wilful urge for freedom and independence that is entirely thwarted by an elevated Saturn in its own sign and conjunct the Midheaven. Although adored in childhood, in latter years she has become a lonely figure, frequently criticized and disapproved of by the public. Her life bears sharp contrast to that of her sister, the Queen, who remains happily married to the man with whom she fell in love and also has the adoration of her people. 'A life doomed to be unfulfilled' as one journalist wrote of her in a recent biography, and certainly the power of this Grand Cross flanking the Ascendant/Descendant and M.C./I.C. axis bears this out.

It is highly tempting to fall back on the idea that karma accounts for the unhappy experiences these two women have encountered in their lives. In many ways, Saturn as the 'Lord of Karma' in such a dominant position in both charts can be seen as an all-seeing judge, meting out pain and difficulty as penalties for previous follies. Yet the emotional and behavioural patterns formed in childhood are clearly implicated in each woman's later problems. Princess Margaret, with her Sun/Neptune conjunction in Leo, adored her father, idealized him and placed him on a pedestal. Consequently her projection of his qualities on to her partners never allowed her to perceive them for themselves, resulting in dissatisfaction and disappointment in her relationships. Elaine's experience of her father resulted in her equating love with pain, a factor which subconsciously coloured her later adult relationships.

In conclusion, the charts of both Princess Margaret and Elaine aptly illustrate the way relationships become the arena for the individual to work out conflicts within herself (or himself) and the way partners become pegs for the individual's own unrecognized qualities. Elaine seeks power and success in her partners as well as compassion and sensitivity (Neptune-ruled seventh house and Moon trine Neptune). As a predominantly earthy person herself, she exudes qualities of efficiency, practicality and capability, all of which her partners found attractive. Water, however is weak in her chart (Jupiter and Pluto are the only planets in this element) and despite a Grand Trine in the water houses (involving Moon and Neptune) the feeling side of her nature has not been allowed full expression. Thus her feelings are in an almost childlike state. By far the most dominant themes in her relationships have been Neptunian and these qualities combined with those of a lack of water have been powerful projections on to her partners. Now, however, these aspects of her own psyche are surfacing. At the moment she is confronted by an overwhelming desire to throw off her cloak of efficiency and capability and immerse herself in the spiritual. She has developed a keen interest in the metaphysical and through meditation is exploring inner realms. This process is in fact revealing aspects of the feminine, within her own psyche. Ultimately she should be free to seek a partner without the unconscious projection that has caused so many problems.

Princess Margaret, having recently come to terms with the failure of a third, highly controversial relationship with a man seventeen years her junior, finds herself, like Elaine, going through a similar process of self-discovery. In the final words of a recently published biography of her life 'Today Princess Margaret is at last at peace with herself. She is in buoyant spirits, excited at the promise of the future, while the perverse meanderings of fate seem like a foreign country . . .'.

5.
CHART COMPARISON

> If a man lives without inner struggle, if everything happens in him without opposition . . . he will remain such as he is.
>
> *Gurdjieff*

Astrology becomes an art in the interpretation of the horoscope, and although every art requires a technique, the artist must in time absorb the technicalities so that they become instinctive. Thus, to begin with, astrology is very much a step-by-step process, fitting together all the pieces; for instance, Moon in Aries, Moon in Aries in the twelfth house, Moon in Aries in the twelfth house square Jupiter, Moon in Aries in the twelfth house square Jupiter and trine Saturn. Synastry requires exactly the same process of assimilating all the astrological pieces; first the individual charts must be assessed and then the comparison aspects. However, the fact that a technique can be applied to the study of relationships must not be allowed to obscure the fact that the coming together of two individuals involves a 'chemical' and 'spiritual' connection — a blending of each person's essence that is beyond the scope of the birth chart.

So much of what the individual needs to experience on an inner level is reflected in his (or her) relationships. Although difficult, inharmonious contacts may exist between two charts, this does not mean that the relationship cannot be rewarding or fulfilling, or that the two people are not 'meant' for each other. There is no guarantee, either, of the exact duration of a relationship. Two individuals may have good synastry but ultimately separate under some difficult Saturn, Pluto or Uranus transit. Yet another couple will ride through similar transits, emerging stronger and more united. Much depends on the individuals concerned, their level of awareness of their needs and each other's.

Early on in my work as an astrologer, I made an incorrect assumption based on the harmonious synastry between a client,

Claire, and a new man in her life, David. Claire's Moon was on David's Ascendant; David's Sun was on Claire's Venus, both of which are traditionally ideal aspects for harmony and compatibility. There were many harmonious sextiles and trines between their planets and the difficulties that were present were hardly insurmountable. To my gratification David proposed within six weeks of the romance; she accepted, but within another five he had called the whole thing off. After an extensive post-mortem as to the possible planetary culprit, nothing emerged, and indeed David never explained to Claire the reason for his change of heart. It appeared that the relationship had outlived its usefulness in three months, providing the contact and the necessary experience for both.

Examining each chart for the potential in relationships is, as we have already seen, an absolute essential before embarking on the synastry. Another important factor for consideration is the age and history of the people concerned. A twenty-two-year-old female with Venus square a seventh house Saturn marrying another twenty-two year old (who is strongly Jupiterian) does not evoke the same scenario as a forty-year-old divorcee marrying a fifty-five-year-old Capricornian. A Venus/Saturn square is a notoriously troublesome aspect involving some learning experience in relationships and some difficulty in finding equilibrium and happiness in matters of affection. A twenty-two-year-old is highly unlikely to have gained enough experience to shed any light on the inner struggle depicted by this aspect. Nor is a strongly Jupiterian man of the same age exactly descriptive of the father figure frequently protrayed by a seventh-house Saturn. Thus it is more than likely that this partner would be the source of some unhappiness and difficulty and that the relationship itself would be subject to considerable growing pains.

Maturity is no guarantee of self-knowledge of course, but Saturn has much to do with this process. About the twenty-ninth year of life (and the fifty-eighth to sixtieth years as well) Saturn returns to its natal position, having transited the twelve signs of the zodiac in its orbit around the Sun. As it reaches this point the full effects of natal Saturn (including all its aspects) are brought into focus. Invariably this involves some difficult outer experiences that allow the individual (with insight and reflection) to understand many of the deeper factors that govern his (or her) life and behaviour. The Saturn Return marks not only the ending of one major life cycle, but the beginning of another, so it is not surprising that many relationships 'go under' at one or both partner's Saturn Return. The individual may sense that he (or she) is at a turning-point and what has been valid and necessary up to this point is not so now. Almost all relationships formed before the Saturn Return go through a period of adjustment at this point. Conversely many people actually marry on or around their twenty-ninth year of life.

It is generally appreciated that people marry for a variety of reasons — some for security or to escape a miserable home life and others for companionship or shared interests. Usually, however people marry for love, which does not always come with a life-long guarantee. One of the points discussed in Chapter 4 was the use of two words for love in Greek, 'eros' (physical and romantic love) and 'agape' (a deep, almost spiritual bond), different experiences which could be correlated to those indicated by Venus and the Moon respectively. Many relationships are initially formed through the eros-Venus expression but not all make the transition to the deeper, more lasting level of 'agape' — one of the reasons why the Moon contacts are so important in synastry.

Once the two charts have been explored for the natal potential in relationships and all the other considerations (background, age, etc.) taken into account, the actual comparison of one chart with another can begin.[1]

Does Each Chart Reflect the Qualities Sought by the Other?

From childhood each individual forms an image of his (or her) ideal man or woman. As we have seen in some of the earlier sections, mother and father present our first important models of male and female and colour our expectations in future relationships. Our imagination, fairy tales and the media do the rest. We want our partners to fulfil our desires and needs and although we may be drawn to people for the qualities we admire, we can also see that our partners become 'pegs' for all our unwanted or unrecognized qualities as well. In Jungian psychology, the animus and anima represent the unconscious male and female figures that we carry within our psyche. Many factors contribute to these images and many of the qualities of the anima and animus can be seen in different areas of the horoscope. Although this may be somewhat of an over-simplification, in a woman's chart the male qualities of the animus can be seen through the masculine planets, particularly the Sun and Mars, and those of the anima through the feminine symbols, especially the Moon and Venus. The state of being 'in love' is often no more than infatuation which frequently involves

[1]As the element interchange has been fully discussed in Chapter 1, reference to this facet of synastry will not be made in this chapter.

the projection of the qualities of the animus/anima on to the partner. This can be a considerable problem if the partner does not measure up to the projection in reality. Ideally each individual needs to recognize the male or female aspects in his (or her) own psyche so that partners do not delude themselves or each other.

The symbols in a horoscope represent the many levels of the individual's being including the prototype of the partner. Thus it is exceedingly important that the partner's chart reflects the qualities sought by the other (and vice versa). For instance, one partner (male) whose Mars is in Aquarius reflects the chart of a female whose Sun is in Aquarius and who also has a Mars/Uranus conjunction in Gemini; the female partner who has Moon in the seventh house reflects the male's Ascendant in Cancer. As I discussed earlier in the chapter in reference to the two females with Venus/Saturn squares, such an aspect can also tell us something about the partner. The Sun, Moon, Venus and Mars, as the principle male/female symbols in a chart, are key factors in showing needs and desires in relationships. Aspects to these planets besides representing character traits and dimensions of the individual's psyche, also describe a type of experience sought in relationships. Thus a partner reflecting these qualities is in a sense helping the individual to relate to this aspect in his (or her) own psyche.

Similar configurations and aspects in one chart and another can be seen to reflect each other as well. In this way two people may have Moon/Pluto squares or the same planet rising; perhaps a Venus/Jupiter conjunction in one chart and a Mars/Jupiter in another. In Figures 4 and 5 (pp. 36 and 37), both partners can be seen to have Venus/Saturn squares in their natal charts. Venus is the ruler of both maps and Saturn is the Sun ruler of John's whereas Mary's Sun ruler, Mars, is conjunct Saturn. Mary has Jupiter conjunct the Ascendant and John has a Sun/Jupiter conjunction. In Figures 12 and 13, both individuals have Moon, Venus oppositions flanking the Ascendant/Descendant axis. Clark Gable has a Moon/Saturn opposition whilst Carole Lombard has an opposition of Sun and Saturn. Lombard has a 'T'-square involving Uranus, Neptune and the Sun (in the fifth, eleventh and eighth houses) and Gable has a similarly positioned 'T'-square involving Uranus, Pluto and Mars. In Figures 14 and 15, Lauren Bacall has a Mars/Neptune opposition and Humphrey Bogart a Venus/Neptune opposition. In Figures 6 and 7 (pp. 39 and 40), Olivier has a Mars/Uranus conjunction and Vivien Leigh one between Moon and Uranus. Both have a Mars/Jupiter oppositions. In particular, it is interesting to note that Gable's Moon/Saturn

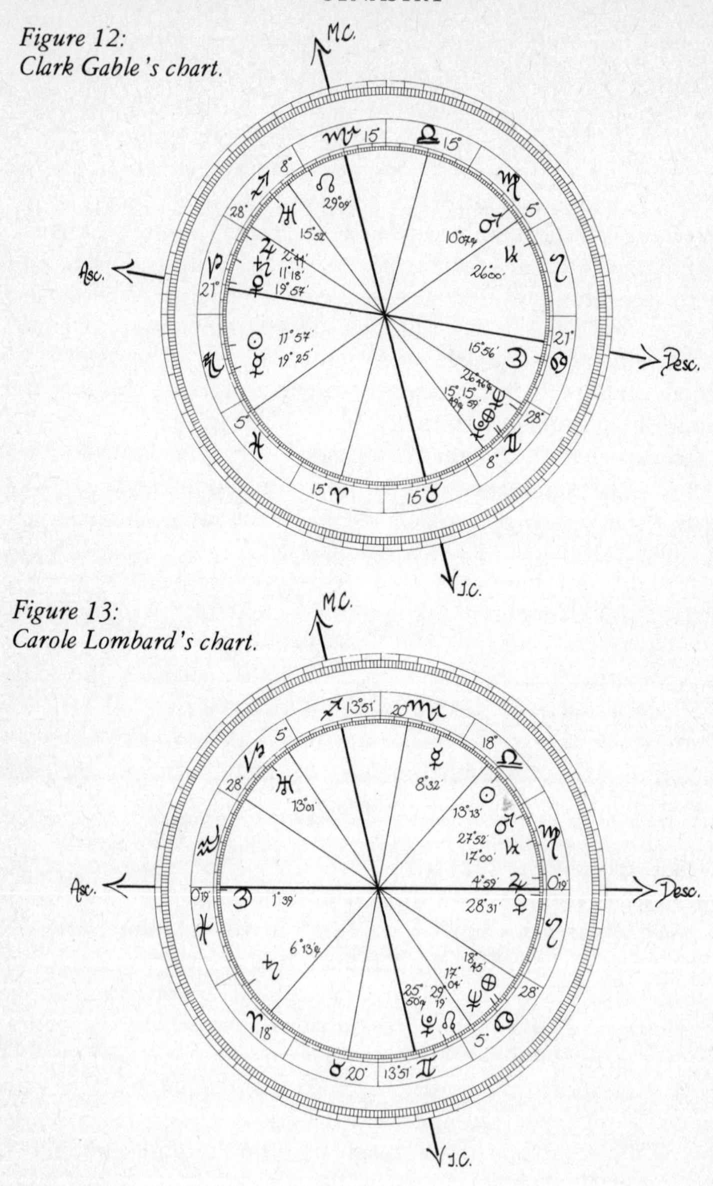

Figure 12:
Clark Gable's chart.

Figure 13:
Carole Lombard's chart.

opposition is reflecting the Feminine, whilst Lombard's Sun/Saturn opposition reflects the Masculine. This same idea can be seen with Bacall's Mars/Neptune opposition and Bogart's Venus/Neptune opposition.

To a certain extent, with similar themes in each individual chart, the relationship becomes a medium for the expression of the actual

Figure 14:
Humphrey Bogart's chart.

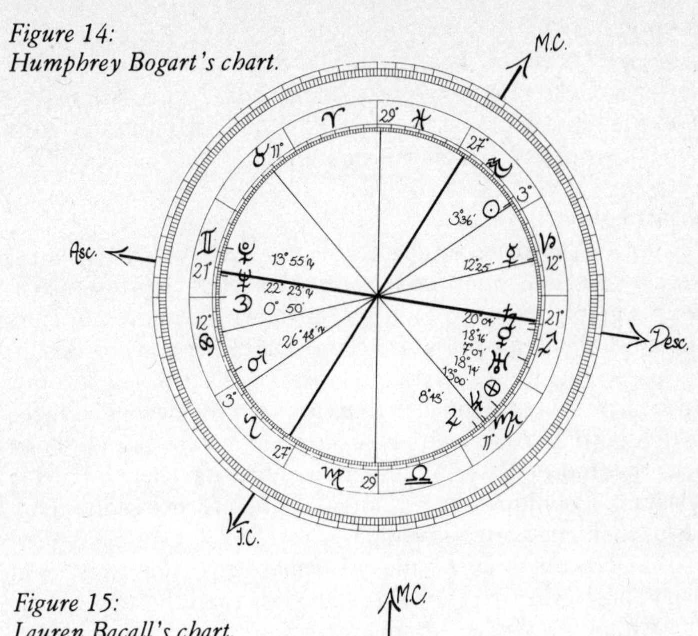

Figure 15:
Lauren Bacall's chart.

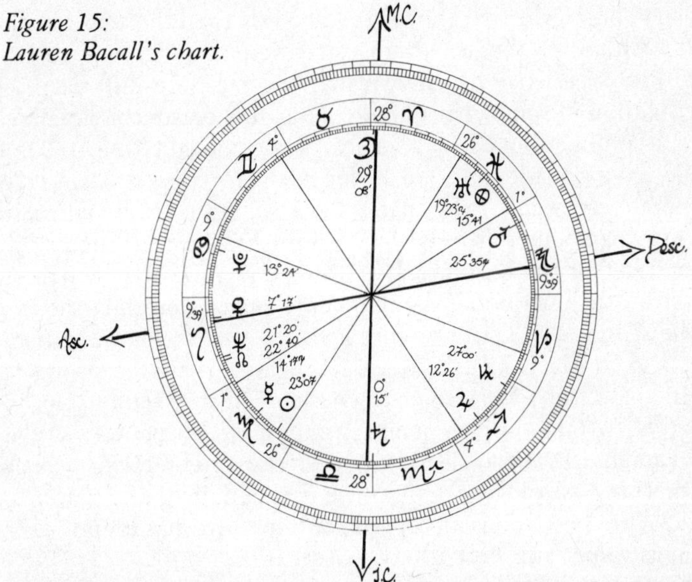

potential, and even if the synastry is difficult, the relationship can still be valid and workable. In fact if two people have similar stressful aspects they can strongly identify with each other's difficulties in the area under focus. Thus such a relationship offers great opportunities to recognize these difficult psychological patterns and learn how best to handle them. Of course, if one dislikes something in oneself, which one then sees in another, it is often difficult to know how to handle this mirror-image. It can easily forge alienation between partners, but as stressful aspects contain the most potential for growth, shared difficulties give the greatest opportunity for self-transmutation.

Inter-aspects

Some contacts between two charts are immediately obvious, whilst others are more difficult to uncover. For this reason it is essential to draw up a graph of the inter-aspects, as shown in Figure 16. Here one can see the inter-aspects between Adolf Hitler and Eva Braun. The closest and most important aspects are encircled to draw attention to the most significant links between the two individuals, thus highlighting major features of the relationship. The closer an aspect, the more powerful and influential its effect. Thus a Mars/Uranus conjunction within a degree is markedly more powerful than one within seven.

Astrologers differ as to the allowable orbs[2] for aspects in synastry, but agree that they should be less than those in a natal chart. Although the orbs suggested here may appear rather generous, experience has shown that wider aspects still have an effect (although somewhat muted). Thus it is reasonable to allow 7° for a conjunction, 6° for a square, opposition and trine, 4° for a sextile, 2° for a quincunx and 1° for the minor aspects. Using the comparatively wider orbs that I have suggested will naturally produce many inter-aspects that, admittedly, can be confusing, particularly for the beginner. By cutting down the orbs by half — 5° for the conjunction, 4° for the square, opposition and trine, 3° for the sextile and 1° for anything else — one is left with fewer aspects to consider. Yet these remaining aspects are the strongest and therefore the most dynamic 'energies' in the relationship. In Figure 16 (p. 91), the closest and strongest aspects between Adolf Hitler and Eva Braun are listed for easier assessment. Poetic licence is something astrologers tend to use occasionally (particularly in considering the viability of aspects) but until one has found one's feet in astrology it is better to use closer orbs.

The first consideration of any aspect is the basic nature of the planets concerned. Harmonious sextiles and trines (and sometimes the conjunctions and oppositions) tend to bring out the positive qualities of the combination, whereas the square, opposition and quincunx aspects inevitably involve some difficulty between the

[2] The distance within which an aspect is judged to be effective.

two principles. The conjunction between two individuals' planets is the strongest contact of all, but sometimes the most insignificant semi-sextile inter-aspect can trigger a major configuration in another's chart (if the aspect is close enough). So, sifting through the aspects carefully is essential.

People born in the same year are bound to have similar aspects between the slower moving planets, so that one person's Pluto conjunct another's merely endorses the collective principle of that planet. However, one person's Pluto conjunct another's Moon has far more powerful and personal implications. In this case the intense energy of Pluto (in one partner) is interacting with the other's feelings and instinctive behaviour (Moon). Thus, the Pluto individual has the ability to evoke a powerful, emotional response in the Moon partner; or to manipulate and dominate him (or her). There is a further point to consider when the two partners are born within the same year. Saturn, Uranus, Neptune and Pluto and sometimes Jupiter are going to be found in roughly the same positions. Thus, when these planets in one partner's chart are aspecting personal planets or points in another, they are reinforcing the natal potential of the aspects — effects with which the individual is already familiar. When the two partners have more than two or three years between them the same factor will not apply (except perhaps with Pluto and Neptune), so any inter-aspects are likely to have more dynamic effects.

Obviously all the inter-aspects have a part to play in synastry but some are more significant than others and will therefore predominate. In Chapter 4, the importance of the Ascendant/Descendant and M.C./I.C. axes was discussed and indeed aspects to these points are *always* significant in relationships. The aspect formed between the Ascendant (or Descendant) ruler of one partner and the Ascendant (or Descendant) ruler of the other is exceedingly important. In fact, if the two planets concerned are in trine and sextile (and sometimes the conjunction and opposition, depending on the planets themselves)[3] it is an excellent indication of happiness and compatibility between the two. When the two planets are in square or quincunx, the contact remains significant but it is less propitious. An aspect may not always be found between the rulers of either of these two points of course, but as this area is a primary factor in relationships, the interplay between signs and

[3] Venus and Jupiter, for instance, are compatible themes even in tense aspect with one another, whereas Mars and Saturn can be difficult to combine harmoniously.

planets here is exceedingly significant for attraction and compatibility. For instance, one partner may have Aquarius rising and the other Uranus conjunct the Ascendant; one partner may have the Descendant in Virgo and the other have the Sun in that sign. Lois Sargent, in her book *How to Handle your Human Relations* gives extensive coverage to these kind of permutations.

There is no such thing as perfect synastry. There are *bound* to be in-harmonious and difficult aspects between a couple as well as harmonious ones and each relationship must be judged on its own merit with all the individual needs and circumstances taken into consideration. However, when there is a predominance of difficult aspects, although the relationship may still 'survive' it is likely to be an uphill struggle for the two people concerned.

The balance of stressful and harmonious aspects between a couple can be ascertained by examining the relevant aspects from the inter-aspect grid (Figure 16) — the harmonious aspects are shown with a tick, the difficult with a cross and the indeterminate with a crossed tick, a total of 19 difficult aspects, 22 harmonious aspects and 11 which are problematic but minor. The qualities of the planets themselves determine the relative ease or difficulty of an aspect which can best be illustrated by example. Hitler's Venus is square to Eva's Sun, but as these two principles are inherently sympathetic, the aspect can be considered as stressful but not seriously undermining to the relationship. In this case the contact between Venus and the Sun suggests that Eva's basic temperament may have been at odds with Hitler's ideal of erotic love and there may have been some disparity between their cultural and social biases. In fact, Hitler's love of the arts was paramount in his life whereas Eva was considerably less *au fait* with most cultural and artistic concerns. As their relationship progressed, however, Eva made a determined effort to acquire knowledge in this area.

Sun/Venus contacts between a couple (particularly when the conjunction, trine, sextile and opposition are involved) are excellent indicators of attraction and affection. Indeed, one of the indicators of the ideal partner is when the female's Sun falls on the male's Venus (and vice versa). Even the more stressful quincunx and square aspects between these two planets can indicate attraction, but then it is frequently accompanied by some difficulties in finding equilibrium in the relationship. Another indication of the ideal partner is when the male's Sun falls on the female's Mars (and vice versa). Mars (and the Sun) in a female's chart describe (amongst other things) the qualities she seeks in a man. When a man's Sun falls on the female's Mars (or Sun) he is

Figure 16:

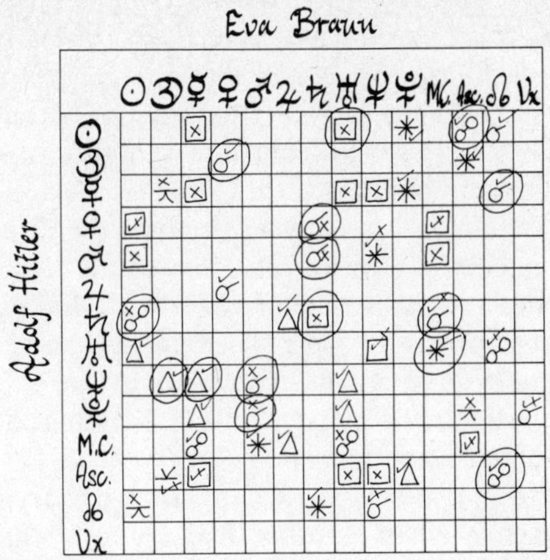

Eva Braun

Adolf Hitler

	☉	☽	☿	♀	♂	♃	♄	♅	♆	♇	M.C.	Asc.	☊	Vx
☉			□					□		✱		☍	☌	
☽				☌								✱		
☿		⚻	□					□	□	✱			☌	
♀	□						☌				□			
♂	□						☌		✱		□			
♃				☌										
♄	☍					△	□				☌			
♅	△								□		✱		☍	
♆		△	△		☌			△						
♇			△		☌			△				⚻		☌
M.C.			☍		✱	△		☍				□		
Asc.		⚻	□					□	□	△			☍	
☊	⚻						✱		☌					
Vx														

Adolf

His ☉ □ her ☿
□ her ♅ (within 27mins.)
✱ her ♇
☌ her Desc.

His ☽ ☌ her ♀
✱ her Asc.

His ☿ □ her ☿
□ her ♆
✱ her ♇
☌ her ☊

His ♀ ☌ her ♄
□ her M.C.

His ♂ ☌ her ♄
□ her M.C. (within 4mins.)

His M.C. ☍ her ♅
□ her Asc.

His Asc. □ her ♅
□ her ♆
△ her ♇
☍ her ☊

His ☊ ✱ her ♄
☌ her ♆

Eva

Her ☉ □ his ♀ (within 1½ degrees.)
□ his ♂
☍ his ♄
△ his ♅

Her ☽ ⚻ his ☿
△ his ♆

Her ☿ △ his ♆
□ his Asc.

Her ♀ ☌ his ♃ (within 16 mins.)

Her ♂ ☌ his ♆
☌ his ♇
✱ his M.C.

Her M.C. ☌ his ♄
✱ his ♅

Her Asc. ⚻ his ♇ (☌ her 8th house cusp)

Her ☊ ☍ his ♅
☌ his Desc.

directly answering these needs; likewise with Venus (and the Moon) in a man's chart. Sun and Mars inter-aspects are not always ideal, however. As can be seen in the inter-aspect grid (Fig. 16), Hitler's Mars is in square aspect to Eva's Sun. This is an aggressive contact between two individuals involving the assertive, demanding, desirous qualities of one person's Mars in conflict with the self-expression of the other. Although the stressful aspects between one person's Mars and another's Sun can be exceedingly difficult to handle, the harmonious aspects are highly productive. The sextile and trine inter-aspect between Sun and Mars indicate that both partners' energy drives complement each other so there is much accomplished when the two work together, and less competitive and quarrelsome tendencies.

The signs the Sun and Moon occupy in each chart and the interchange between them is another major consideration in chart comparison. In regarding the Sun and Moon contacts between a couple, whether it be Sun/Sun; Sun/Moon, or Moon/Moon, because of the importance of these two planetary bodies, even if no actual aspect is formed, the respective signs, elements and qualities should be carefully considered.

The Sun

The two Suns indicate how the couple operate on an outer level. Aspects formed between the Sun of one partner and the planets of another show how the latter supports and respects the partner as an individual and how he (or she) encourages and sympathizes with the aims and temperament of the partner. Having two Suns in harmonious signs is a good indicator of compatibility, but the fact that they fall in discordant signs is not the most difficult obstacle to overcome in a relationship. As was discussed in Chapter 1, there is a definite attraction between antithetical signs of the same quality, and although inevitably their personalities clash at times, harmonious links elsewhere in the synastry help offset any deep conflict. Of course, if there are many difficulties in the synastry, disparate Sun signs are a distinct disadvantage.

With Hitler's and Eva's Suns in fixed signs, stubbornness and rigidity were qualities they both shared. Eva's Aquarian disposition was detached and unpredictable, whereas Hitler's Taurean nature would have been more reserved and patient. When Suns are found in square aspect to each other or in square signs, the individuals may be perennially at cross purposes. But providing there are other harmonious inter-aspects with the Sun and Moon, this is not an insurmountable obstacle to shared happiness. Suns in opposition attract or repel, whereas the sextile and trine indicate balanced and harmonizing temperaments.

The Sun and Moon

The contacts between the Suns and Moons of two people are prime indicators of the degree of basic psychological and emotional compatibility between a couple. The Sun as the masculine 'dominant' principle is naturally complemented by the feminine receptivity of the Moon. In fact, the classic significator of harmony between a couple is when the Moon of the female partner is conjunct the male's Sun. This is also true in reverse when the male's Moon is conjunct the female's Sun.[4] The conjunction is the most powerful aspect, of course, but a close sextile or trine aspect between the Sun of one partner and the Moon of the other can also indicate attraction, harmony and compatibility. The signs the Sun and Moon are placed in are exceedingly important factors for consideration. Even if no actual aspect is formed between these two planetary bodies the interchange of the signs, elements and qualities throws much light on the relationship. Thus if one partner has his Sun in an air sign and the other the Moon in air or fire, even without the presence of an exact aspect, the signs and elements can be seen to be complementary. *In the example chart comparison we have been using, there is no aspect formed between Eva's and Hitler's Sun and Moon nor any aspect between Sun and Sun or Moon and Moon. However, Eva's Moon in Virgo complements Hitler's earthy Taurean Sun, giving some indication of compatibility.*

The opposition of one partner's Sun and the other's Moon frequently acts as an attraction mechanism between a couple, but the square, although a strong attraction feature initially, invariably causes problems later in the relationship. The partner whose Moon is squared by the other's Sun may find him (or her) dominating and insensitive whilst the Sun individual feels the Moon partner is oversensitive and emotional. This is reminiscent of the dilemma between the fire/water couple which has been covered in Chapter 2.

[4] Carl Jung, as part of his lifelong interest in astrology researched five hundred married couples, using their birth charts to test these classic aspects. He found a significant proportion had Sun conjunct Moon, Moon conjunct Moon or Moon conjunct Ascendant. He reported his findings in his monograph, *Synchronicity — An Acausal Connecting Principle.*

The Sun and Uranus, Neptune and Pluto

Aspects from the outer planets of one partner to the Sun of another are always interesting and usually powerful. Uranus contacts frequently involve sudden, magnetic attractions (particularly conjunctions). Uranus has great charisma for the Sun; thus, the partner whose Uranus is aspecting the other's Sun challenges and awakens him (or her), although if there is a surfeit of Uranus contacts, the relationship may be rather unpredictable and short-lived. An individual whose Sun is aspected by another's Neptune is often enthralled by the Neptune partner, who inspires and empathizes with him (or her). Neptune can indicate a heightened spiritual feeling between two people, but it must be remembered that Neptune's other face is one of deception and confusion, so the Neptune partner can let the other down or even undermine his self-respect and confidence. Pluto contacts from one individual to another's Sun are profound and transforming. The Pluto partner stimulates much growth in the Sun individual on an inner and outer level. As any Pluto contact to a personal planet tends to be somewhat intense, these contacts either considerably raise the level of the relationship, or indicate the presence of ego-conflicts and power struggles.

In the inter-aspect example, it can be seen that Eva's Uranus forms an exact square to Hitler's Sun, while Hitler's Uranus trines Eva's. This suggests that in Eva's case, Hitler awakened her creative potential and brought out new dimensions in her personality. Consequently she may have blossomed through the relationship. However, as Eva's Uranus forms a tense aspect to Hitler's Sun, perhaps we can see here that her unpredictable temperament (amplified by her Aquarian Sun and Moon/Uranus trine) created tension and impatience in Hitler, which may well have been ultimately detrimental to his leadership image. Eva's Pluto, however, counteracts some of these inflammatory tendencies by forming a harmonious sextile to Hitler's Sun. This suggests that Eva could well have stimulated Hitler's ambitions and encouraged him to have faith in his visions and develop his personal power!

Moon and Moon

As far as marriage, or any long-term emotional partnership is concerned, the most important planetary relationship to consider is that of the respective Moons. The Moon is instinctual and responsive; it shows how each individual feels and senses. It also represents unconscious and deep-seated emotional patterns. When the two Suns are in conflicting signs, the two individuals may experience personality clashes but they are externalized and easier to deal with. The Moons, when found in conflicting signs and forming a difficult aspect, are a different matter altogether. When this occurs neither partner feels truly 'at home' with the other. The emotional response needed by each individual is not answered by the other and because this is a non-rational and entirely subjective experience for each partner, no amount of discussion or objective reasoning can alter the situation. When the Moons are in conjunction, and even when they occupy the same sign, both partners sense they 'belong' to each other. With compatible Moon signs and harmonious aspects between the Moons, adjustments are easier to make in the relationship. *Using our example comparison, Hitler's Moon and Eva's Moon, although not in trine aspect to each other, are none the less in harmonious earth signs, which indicates a certain harmony and adaptability to each other. Thus, there was likely to be much sympathy and agreement underlying the complexity of their relationship.*

In my own work, I have found couples with excellent synastry between them who, because the Moons were in difficult aspect to one another and in conflicting signs, never felt complete with each other; and, likewise, couples with many difficult inter-aspects to contend with, and who have experienced much challenge and difficulty in their relationship, nevertheless have had a rich and satisfying emotional bond with each other, when their Moons were conjunct.

By far the most powerful link between Moons is when they are conjunct and in the same sign. On a peripheral level, this indicates that the couple instinctively adapt to, agree and co-operate with each other. However, there are deeper implications. The Moon represents the past and memories we hold buried deep in our unconscious. Although Moons conjunct or in the same sign indicate there may be a sense of common origins or a shared background, these origins may extend beyond the borders of the present lifetime. Some astrologers feel that couples who have their Moons conjunct (or in the same sign) have had a relationship in a previous existence and that this sense of belonging, love at first sight, instant recognition and feeling of familiarity has its roots in a distant past.

Moons in opposition may indicate that there are differences in emotional patterns and in feelings generally, but there is considerable compatibility shown here as well as much give-and-take between a couple. The square and quincunx cause misunderstandings and emotional dis-ease between two individuals. Unless there are good aspects between Moon and Venus, there may be considerable insensitivity to each other and some irritability and tension.

Moon and Mercury

One of the most helpful combinations in synastry is a good relationship between one partner's Moon and the other's Mercury. A conjunction between the Moon and Mercury is even better than one between the two Mercuries, but not as powerful as a Moon/Moon conjunction. Moon and Mercury indicate an instinctive understanding between the two individuals and a harmonious aspect between these two planets goes a long way to promote harmony and durability in a relationship, especially when other exceedingly difficult inter-aspects are present. The opposition from one person's Mercury to another's Moon may indicate that the Moon individual finds the Mercury partner too intent on rationalizing the former's feelings rather than relating to them instinctively. Sometimes this aspect can stimulate much creative thought in the lunar partner. With the square and quincunx between Mercury and the Moon in synastry, the Mercury partner may have little regard for the lunar individual's moods and feelings and may actively criticize him (or her), making the Moon partner insecure, nervous and hypersensitive. *Thus, in the example synastry of Hitler and Eva Braun, the close quincunx between Hitler's Mercury and Eva's Moon did little to mitigate their severe differences of opinion as seen through the respective Mercury aspects. In fact, Hitler displayed outright insensitivity to Eva's feelings by refusing to officially acknowledge her position. Through this lack of understanding he made her feel rejected, insecure and unimportant — factors which no doubt contributed to her suicide attempts.*

Moon and Venus

In a marriage or any loving relationship, good aspects between these feminine planets are an enormous help. With the conjunction, sextile or trine aspect, there is much consideration, love and devotion to one another. In fact, harmonious aspects between Moon and Venus are good indicators of a happy marriage. Even when there are some exceedingly difficult inter-aspects elsewhere in the synastry, this gentle and loving combination of planets does much to soften any conflict and disagreement. The opposition between these two planets can indicate a strong attraction and a loving bond between two people, but the square and quincunx can cause a certain awkwardness in expressing joint feelings easily. However, as with the 'hard' Sun/Venus inter-aspects, those between Moon and Venus will not seriously undermine the relationship, unless there is much affliction elsewhere in the synastry.

In the case of Hitler and Eva Braun, one of the most encouraging factors in the relationship was the conjunction of Eva's Venus to Hitler's Moon/Jupiter conjunction. Much mutual affection and sympathy is designated here and indeed much happiness. In fact, this aspect does much to alleviate many of the more uncomfortable contacts that we shall cover shortly and certainly supplies us with a reason why and how the relationship lasted until their deaths — a period of some sixteen years.

Moon and Mars

Moon and Mars inter-aspects can stimulate sexual attraction between a couple, yet this combination can also provoke arguments and disagreements, particularly when in square and quincunx. The partner whose Mars aspects the other's Moon may be over-forceful and demanding on the emotions of the lunar individual, and whether for good or bad, the Mars partner certainly arouses the Moon's feelings. Venus and Mars contacts seem to have a better avenue for expression in the physical aspect of a relationship, whereas the Moon is perhaps rather oversensitive and easily hurt by the 'pushy', desirous nature of Mars. This can lead to the Moon person deliberately rejecting any sexual response from the Mars partner. The conjunction is particularly potent in the physical exchange between a couple, and the sextile and trine bode well for co-operation in shared activities.

The Moon and Uranus, Neptune and Pluto

Moon/Uranus contacts between a couple trigger much initial attraction. The Uranus partner fascinates and excites the lunar individual and opens up a new dimension in his emotional expression. As with all contacts from this outer planet to the personal areas and planets of another, the possibilities of gaining emotionally in new and unusual ways is counterbalanced by the equally unstable and erratic tendencies of Uranus. The partner whose Moon is in square, quincunx, opposition or conjunction to the other's Uranus may feel in a permanent state of high tension in the presence of that partner. Uranus lends much stimulation to a relationship in small doses, but its difficulties tend to emerge in the long term. Although a Moon/Uranus square between a couple is unlikely to cause a major stumbling block in a relationship, if this contact is accompanied by many other Uranus inter-aspects, it is likely that the couple will need plenty of breathing space between them and, perhaps, periods of separation. Otherwise, it is rather like overloading a power circuit.

With Moon/Neptune contacts a couple can feel psychically in tune with each other. The Neptune partner intuitively understands the moods and reactions of the other, and for this reason the lunar individual can become exceedingly emotionally dependent on the former. The conjunction is the most powerful indicator of a psychic tie, but all aspects with Neptune have this potential. Neptune can of course be elusive and devious. Thus, with the square, opposition, quincunx, and sometimes the conjunction, there is a possibility that misunderstandings and deception will be provoked by the Neptune partner.

Moon/Pluto inter-aspects can be constructive or destructive depending on the nature of the individuals concerned. The Pluto partner has the ability to touch the Moon individual at a deep level which can be a transforming experience or a traumatic one. The square, quincunx, opposition (and sometimes the conjunction) can indicate that the Pluto partner is intensely possessive of the Moon individual and emotionally manipulative. The trine and sextile are more conducive to the transforming qualities of this combination.

In the synastry between Hitler and Braun, there is a sympathetic trine aspect formed from Hitler's Neptune to Eva's Moon. This is indeed one of the indicators of a psychic link and of an intuitive understanding of each other's needs that has been mentioned above. Furthermore, Hitler's Neptune forms a Grand Trine to Eva's Moon at 26° 40′ Virgo and her Mercury at 28° 19′ Capricorn, so although Hitler's Neptune is in an air sign (whereas Eva's Moon and Mercury are in earth) there is nevertheless a strong indication that there was much mutual sympathy and tenderness between them.

Venus and Mars

Aspects between Venus and Mars, and from other planets to these two in chart comparison, demonstrate the physical workings of the relationship and how the affections and desires blend and complement each other. Conjunctions, trines and sextiles between these two planets in respective charts bode well for the physical and sexual exchange in marriage. The partner whose Mars is aspecting the other's Venus is likely to stimulate the latter's love nature through his (or her) strong desires, yet the former may also be rather insistent, pushy and possessive. When the square, opposition or quincunx occurs between one partner's Venus and the other's Mars, there is usually just as much physical attraction between the two. In fact, the desires of the Mars partner may be even stronger than with the more harmonious aspects. However, there can be a certain coarseness and harshness about the Mars partner that may attract yet also repel the Venus individual. Sometimes difficult aspects between these two planets cause tension and conflict in the relationship and often some unfaithfulness.

Using our example charts of Hitler and Eva once again, there is a very wide trine aspect between each individual's Venus and another between Hitler's Mars and Eva's Venus. Had the aspect been closer, one might have been persuaded to believe that the physical dimension of their relationship was a sustaining feature and mutually satisfying. However, as both aspects are wide (about eight degrees apart), whilst there is certainly an indication of some physical compatibility (all factors involved are in earth signs) Hitler's Venus/Mars conjunction is restricted by Eva's Saturn. Thus, it is more likely that the physical side of their relationship was less than satisfactory and may actually have been the focus of much frustration and unhappiness. (A fuller explanation given later of the Saturn contacts to Venus and Mars should shed more light on this area of the relationship.)

Venus and Uranus, Neptune and Pluto

Aspects between the Venus of one partner and the Uranus of the other cause some exciting sparks in a relationship. Although Uranus contacts are not exactly a stabilizing feature in synastry, this planet can awaken the nature of any planet it aspects. Thus Uranus stimulates the love nature of Venus and apart from bringing out the creative and the original in this way, this combination often indicates there is something unusual about the relationship itself. The harmonious aspects from Uranus to Venus, and even the conjunction and opposition, can show magnetic attraction between two individuals, and a strong emphasis on romance and excitement. The square and quincunx (and sometimes the opposition and conjunction) give rise to tension, however, and there is a possibility of the Uranus individual being a little too sexually adventurous for the Venus partner. The opposition, quincunx and square may increase any tendencies towards instability and infidelity in the relationship. There needs to be plenty of more stabilizing factors in the synastry with many Uranus contacts between a couple, and stressful Venus/Uranus contacts, including the conjunction, can indicate an erratic and short-lived relationship.

Neptune and Venus inter-aspects are inspiring, sensitive and romantic. The Neptune partner may be capable of great self-sacrifice and utter devotion to the Venus individual. The trine and sextile aspects bring out the best qualities of this dyad; however, the conjunction, square and opposition need careful handling. With the latter aspects, the partner whose Neptune is contacting the other's Venus may initially captivate him (or her) — Neptune is very glamorous and fascinating to Venus — but the Neptune partner may also disappoint and deceive. Particularly when Neptune and Venus are involved in a double interchange (A's Venus aspecting B's Neptune and B's Venus aspecting A's Neptune), the couple may experience states of ecstasy in love. These contacts, rather like those of the Moon and Neptune, can indicate the feeling of having made contact with one's soulmate.

All Pluto contacts to personal planets need assessing carefully. Pluto's extreme nature, with its ability to transform and penetrate, can elevate or degrade the love nature of Venus. Thus, there are individuals who have Venus/Pluto inter-aspects who experience an intense and deep relationship that is fulfilling and enriching to both, and there are others who experience considerable cruelty and trauma. In conjunction, square and opposition, the Pluto individual can be over-possessive and manipulate the Venus partner, who may in turn find the former vulgar, difficult to understand and even degenerate. Pluto and Venus contacts are particularly problematic in the sexual area of the relationship as the Pluto individual may force the Venus partner to comply with his (or her) desires. Harmonious Venus/Pluto aspects indicate strong physical attraction. Infidelities are unlikely to be tolerated in the relationship, particularly by the Pluto partner, although the latter may feel a law unto himself or herself in this respect.

Mars and Uranus, Neptune and Pluto

Uranus aspects from one partner to the other's Mars are infinitely more of a problem than those between Venus and Uranus. The Uranus individual may encourage the Mars partner to 'do his own thing', but unless this aspect is a trine or a sextile this may lead to an inability to compromise or work in tune with one another. With the opposition and the square, there may be considerable intolerance and irritability between the two and many major upheavals and violent quarrels. The conjunction (and to a lesser extent the opposition) of one person's Uranus to another's Mars can be highly sexually exciting but this can also turn into open rebellion. Providing there are other softer aspects between a couple, perhaps some gentle Moon/Venus or Venus/Jupiter ones, Mars/Uranus aspects are stimulating confined to the bedroom. As with all hard

Uranus inter-aspects, the partners need to distance themselves from each other periodically.

Mars/Neptune inter-aspects are nearly always problematic. The exception is when both partners are involved in Neptunian work or have shared Neptunian interests (such as the healing and mystical arts, drama, painting and music, etc.). Neptune has a subtle, debilitating and undermining effect on the energies and desires of Mars, although the sextile and trine can demonstrate sympathy and encouragement in the Neptune partner to the desires of the Mars individual, possibly aiding him intuitively. The conjunction, opposition, quincunx and square, however, can gnaw at the self-confidence of the Mars individual or actively lead him (or her) astray. Sometimes, too, with the more stressful aspects, the Mars individual can inflate the worries of the Neptune partner by over-stimulating his imagination. If the two individuals in the relationship already have Neptune strongly featured in their own charts, the added influence of Mars and Neptune in the synastry can weave a web of confusion and misunderstanding over relationship matters and each other.

When the Pluto of one partner forms an aspect to another's Mars, the former has a tendency to feel somewhat threatened by the 'fire' of the Mars individual. Thus the Pluto partner may try to control and dictate to the Mars individual, who naturally rebels. Physical clashes frequently occur with Mars/Pluto contacts, particularly in square and opposition, whereas the sextile or trine, and sometimes the conjunction, can strengthen the combined wills of the couple. Mars/Pluto contacts, like those of Venus/Pluto, have a strong sexual connotation, so that the inter-aspects demonstrate the level and intensity of the physical attraction between a couple. Care needs to be taken in releasing the Plutonian energy in small doses, otherwise the intensity can be overwhelming and possibly even destroy the relationship.

The comparison example shows that there are no Venus inter-aspects with Uranus, Neptune and Pluto. However, Hitler's Neptune forms a close conjunction to Eva's Mars, whilst Eva's Neptune is in wide sextile to Hitler's Mars. Neither party was involved in the healing arts and as we have seen with the Sun/Venus square Hitler and Eva had disparate cultural and artistic inclinations. The Mars/Neptune inter-aspects could perhaps indicate a shared interest in mystical pursuits. There appears to be some confusion about whether or not Hitler had taken astrological advice during his leadership, particularly as astrology was officially condemned in 1941. Yet the use of the occult symbol, the swastika, and the fact that several of his colleagues (including Goebels) were known to dabble in the occult, leads one to believe that he may have had more than a passing interest in such things. Thus it is just feasible that Eva and Hitler dabbled in some strange practices and that Eva's Neptune may have sympathized with his beliefs and aided his ambitions with her intuitive perception! Hitler's Neptune on Eva's Mars is a close aspect and therefore more 'influential'. The Neptune partner can be very deceptive and evasive to the Mars individual which in this case can be seen in the way he avoided marriage to Eva until quite literally the last moment. However, perhaps here we also see that he may have made her unable to act as she wanted; his presence may have disarmed her intentions and clouded her sense of direction as so often happens with Mars/Neptune contacts.

Mercury

Communication is an essential ingredient for the success of a relationship. Even if two people have difficulty in intuitively responding to one another's feelings or understanding each other's habits and ways of doing things, provided they communicate with each other, there is an opportunity for things to be worked out. Thus, Mercury aspects in synastry are of great importance. If the two partners' Mercuries are in conflicting signs and form inharmonious aspects, not only are they likely to reason things out in totally different ways, but their actual perception of the world is radically different. In consequence, with different values and different views on how to tackle issues and approach decisions, many difficulties and much argument arise in relationships.

Whilst conflicting Mercuries can be a problem between any two people, when there is no meeting of minds in a marriage where everyday decisions (as well as crucial ones) have to be made, every issue is a potential source of disagreement. If both people have different perspectives, they may communicate, but neither understands the other or feels his (or her) viewpoint is valid. Consequently both individuals become closed to each other and communication on all levels breaks down. With the cardinal and mutable Mercuries, there is a tendency to spar continually and make cutting remarks about each other.

The strength and importance of Mercury aspects are sometimes overlooked in chart comparison in favour of the Sun, Moon, Venus and Mars contacts, but great attention should be paid to the contact between the two Mercuries and any inter-aspects with other planets. The squares between Mercuries are most stressful, particularly in fixed signs, when the added dimension of stubbornness impedes any compromise. Criticism and lack of appreciation for each other's ideas and opinions can frustrate both individuals, and constant disagreement and carping will eventually wear down any relationship. As Mercury is never further than 28° from the Sun, Mercury squares invariably involve the Suns as well, which adds to the general picture of discomfort. With a change of sign or lack of conjunction between the Sun and Mercury, the problem is lessened. Even without a square aspect actually being involved in the synastry, with the Mercuries in conflicting signs there is still a totally different process of thinking demonstrated by each partner. A slight exception here is when the Mercuries are in air and earth signs, as both these elements share a rational quality. Opposing Mercuries can stimulate a healthy objectivity between a couple. Conjunctions are an excellent pointer for compatibility and indicate that the couple share many views, so that there is likely to be much mutual understanding and agreement.

Mercury and Uranus, Neptune and Pluto

The aspects from one partner's Uranus or Pluto to the other's Mercury have both mentally stimulating and disturbing effects. Uranus in tense aspect to another's Mercury may highlight radical differences of opinion and exceedingly different personal views. Arguments tend to arise out of nowhere and the Uranian partner may refuse to listen to the Mercury individual. Harmonious sextile and trine aspects between Mercury and Uranus can indicate a telepathic understanding of each other and the Uranus partner may broaden the Mercury individual's mentality and encourage unusual interests.

Harmonious sextiles and trines between Mercury and Neptune (and sometimes the conjunction and opposition) also indicate a certain telepathic understanding between a couple. The squares, however, may mean that the Neptune partner is prone to lying to the Mercury individual, or confusing him (or her) and blurring his (or her) ability to reason.

The individual whose Pluto forms difficult aspects to the other's Mercury (square, opposition, quincunx and sometimes the conjunction) may force his opinions on the partner and subtly manipulate his (or her) thinking processes. This also indicates possible mental cruelty. With the sextile and trine aspect, however, the Pluto individual can lead the Mercury partner to greater understanding of himself (or herself) and transform his ideas.

With the example comparison, Hitler and Eva Braun have their

Mercuries in square signs and in close square aspect to each other. The Uranus/Mercury square in their synastry suggests that although Hitler found Eva a highly stimulating companion, she also had the ability to irritate and aggravate him. No doubt Hitler, with both Sun and Mars in immovable Taurus, found Eva unstable, erratic and volatile on occasion (Eva's natal Moon trine Uranus and Mercury conjunct Uranus). Added to this, Eva's Neptune squaring Hitler's Mercury could have created much confusion in his mind. This combined with the conflicting Mercuries themselves may have resulted in frequent misunderstandings and communication breakdowns. The difficulties may have been somewhat eased by Hitler's Neptune/Pluto conjunction in trine to Eva's Mercury, and Eva's Pluto forming a sextile with Hitler's Mercury. Neptune/Mercury trines tend to reinforce the idea of a psychic link between two people, with the Neptune partner (in this case Hitler) inspiring and encouraging the Mercury individual (Eva) to widen her perceptions. Good aspects from Pluto to both Mercuries (a two-way aspect) indicates that their joint experiences brought about powerful changes in their lives.

Jupiter

Jupiter contacts between a couple boost the relationship on all levels. In the Jupiter section in Chapter 4, I mentioned that without fun, good feelings and the good times, all of which are Jupiterian by nature, relationships would hardly flourish! One person's Jupiter forming aspects with another's Sun, Moon, Mercury and Mars brings out the best qualities of these planets. In fact, Jupiter conjunctions, sextiles and trines put the relationship on to an exceedingly positive footing. Couples who have strong Jupiter inter-aspects enjoy and feel the benefit of each other, which bodes for happy, long-lasting relationships. The presence of one or two harmonious aspects from Jupiter can alleviate many of the difficulties elsewhere in the synastry.

When one person's Jupiter aspects the Sun of another, the Sun partner finds that the Jupiter individual increases his or her self-confidence and may actually encourage financial, material and spiritual growth. It must be remembered, however, that Jupiter can also tend to excess, so sometimes the Jupiter partner (especially when Jupiter is in opposition, square and quincunx to the other's Sun) will try to take over the partner, insisting on his own, usually more extravagant way, at all times. Sun/Jupiter, Moon/Jupiter and Venus/Jupiter aspects expand the loving and exuberant nature of the relationship and indicate good feelings and mutual happiness through the contact with each other. The Jupiter partner is frequently generous, protective and indulgent to the Moon and Venus individual.

Mercury/Jupiter inter-aspects forge mutual growth in all areas, but particularly in attitudes and mental endeavours. Jupiter's optimistic and expressive nature encourages the Mercury individual to think in broad positive terms and there may be joint interest in metaphysical and religious matters. The opposition, square and quincunx can indicate a little too much force on the Jupiter individual's behalf to convert the Mercury partner to all his (or her) beliefs and ideas.

One person's Jupiter contacting another's Mars is likely to stimulate and encourage the ambitions and desires of the Mars partner. Conjunctions, sextiles and trines between Mars and Jupiter, and Venus and Jupiter point to mutually happy and satisfying physical and sexual relationships. The square, opposition and quincunx aspects can sometimes lead to over-indulgence in these areas and with Jupiter in square aspect to Venus there is a tendency for the (Jupiter) partner to over-commit himself or herself financially. Thus, the generosity of Jupiter turns into extravagance and indulgence, which may put the relationship in jeopardy. The Jupiter individual needs to be more considerate of the partner and less forceful in the relationship.

Jupiter and Jupiter, Uranus, Neptune and Pluto

With one person's Jupiter in conjunction, sextile or trine to another's, there is likely to be much agreement and happiness in shared ideals, beliefs, mutual endeavours and pleasures. With the opposition, square and quincunx, although the respective attitude to religion, beliefs and pleasures may differ markedly, these differences are not deeply upsetting to the relationship. However, if there are a great many difficulties in the synastry between two individuals, the inharmonious Jupiter aspects tend to inflate the problems rather than smoothe them over.

Uranus square, opposition and quincunx aspects to another's Jupiter tends to bring out reckless and extravagant urges in the Jupiter partner, whereas the trine, sextile and conjunction can stimulate spiritual and philosophical interests. The Uranus partner can challenge and encourage the Jupiter individual to broaden his belief systems and expand his horizons in every way.

Conjunctions, sextiles and trines between one partner's Neptune and another's Jupiter promotes sensitivity and appreciation of each other's religious and spiritual goals. The conjunction encourages a relationship in which spiritual matters in general and relating to each other on a spiritual level are highly important. The square, quincunx and opposition can indicate that the Neptune partner is not the best person to give practical advice to the Jupiter individual!

Pluto/Jupiter conjunctions, sextiles and trines between a couple encourage tremendous growth and understanding between them. The opposition, quincunx and square (and sometimes the conjunction) show that blocks may occur over beliefs and ideals, which make co-operation and mutual encouragement in this direction exceedingly difficult.

In the inter-aspects between Hitler and Eva Braun, Hitler's Jupiter forms an almost exact conjunction to Eva's Venus. As Eva and Hitler had many difficulties to contend with in their relationship (which can be seen through the Mercury squares and the Uranus, Neptune and Saturn inter-aspects to their personal planets), the Venus/Jupiter contact shows that there were some happier and mutually beneficial energies also at work.

Saturn

The role Saturn plays in relationships is highly significant. In fact in many cases a relationship stands or falls on its ability to incorporate Saturn successfully. Much depends, of course, on the position of this planet in each individual chart. An individual who has many 'hard' Saturn aspects in his horoscope has lived with them all his (or her) life. Thus, if he (or she) forms a relationship involving many Saturn cross-contacts, the relationship in effect, is mirroring the exact requirements of the natal chart. However, if an exceedingly Jupiterian individual finds himself in a relationship full of Saturn difficulties this hardly reflects the expansive, out-pouring nature of Jupiter, so it is more than likely that he will feel constricted and unhappy in the relationship.

Saturn needs to be regarded on two levels to understand its significance in synastry. First as the 'Lord of Time' who set the 'fates' in motion, Saturn can be seen as a central figure in the working out of karmic law. Saturn contacts in synastry show where the two individuals need to work something out together in the way of a karmic debt — hence the inescapable aura about Saturn contacts. Secondly, Saturn represents that which lasts and endures and without Saturn aspects in synastry, a relationship will fall apart at the seams. The Saturn principle of duty and responsibility is clearly present in the legally binding ceremony of marriage — a ceremony which is designed to bond two people together for life.

In her book *Saturn*, Liz Greene states, 'What we tend to forget about relationships is that we do not generally form them for the purpose of being happy; we form them to complete something incomplete . . .'. This statement seems to require some qualification, as most individuals form emotional relationships in definite anticipation of happiness! Perhaps it is necessary to consider that the conscious ideal of happiness is invariably at odds with inner needs, particularly if a person's ideal of happiness is tantamount to having plenty of money and material possessions. Happiness springs from a sense of harmony and balance within oneself — a state requiring self-knowledge and acceptance. Relationships are a process whereby such knowledge is acquired. Thus each partner becomes a source for completing that which is incomplete. It may be labouring the point, but in seeing one's qualities in someone else (particularly those that are disliked), in dealing with them and ultimately in recognizing them as one's own, self-knowledge is gained and a step taken towards creating inner harmony and balance — from which stems happiness! Although one can hardly consider Saturn to be a planet synonymous with the idea of happiness, it is none the less an essential 'door-way' and route towards it. Liz Greene concludes that it is 'this process of mutual growth through the gradual unfolding of self-knowledge that brings the field of human relationships under Saturn's influence'.

Saturn's inter-aspects with the personal planets, the angles and the nodal axis are highly significant in synastry. Individuals with strong Saturn inter-aspects frequently experience a compulsive attraction towards each other that often turns in time into intense dislike. There is a traditional view in astrology that, as the sign and house in which Saturn is placed invariably denotes an area fraught with difficulty for the individual, others with that same sign strongly featured in their own charts are inherently problematic for the individual. In effect, when one partner's personal planets contact the Saturn of the other, they are touching on a highly vulnerable area — an area the partner already treats as alien and fearful in his (or her) own nature. The usual reaction to something that is feared is to flee from it or 'kill it', which symbolically is the reaction Saturn produces when in contact with another's personal planets. Here again, myth can shed some light on Saturn's action in synastry. Saturn's castration of his father (Ouranus) — an action taken to make him all-powerful and invulnerable — is symbolically demonstrated in Saturn's contacts to another's planets. In synastry, Saturn 'castrates' through dismissive criticism, by stifling spontaneity and by engendering worry and insecurity.

Saturn inter-aspects are difficult to handle since instead of forging any direct confrontation, there is a continual wearing down of the partner's confidence (in the area in question) that breeds frustration and resentment.

Sun/Saturn inter-aspects occur with great frequency in relationships. Initially, the Saturn partner is attracted by the qualities of the Sun individual but gradually begins to criticize the partner for those very same qualities. This is particularly true of the conjunction and opposition, or when Saturn is found in the same sign or opposite to that of the partner's Sun. The Saturn individual tends to deflate or dampen the Sun's self-confidence and enthusiasm, which can in time lead the Sun partner to regard the Saturn individual as an authoritarian figure — one to be feared and resented.

Sun/Saturn contacts also indicate durability in a relationship and providing there are some good Moon and Venus inter-aspects, this contact can be a very positive influence in the partnership. The square and quincunx aspects between Sun and Saturn, however, both tend to create conflict in a relationship, with the Saturn partner appearing to hinder and block the actions of the Sun individual. The trine and sextile aspects between Sun and Saturn give substance and integrity to the relationship, although it is just as possible for the Saturn partner to become a constricting influence as it is with the more stressful inter-aspects.

Moon/Saturn contacts are far more problematic in relationships, but again they appear with uncanny frequency in chart comparison. As with the Sun/Saturn inter-aspects, there is every indication that the relationship will endure but at the expense of some emotional constraint. There is a coldness about Moon/Saturn contacts (especially the conjunction), although harshness and emotional distance can also occur with the square, opposition and quincunx. The lunar individual may never feel free to express his feelings in Saturn's presence and may find that he is expected to control his emotions. The Saturn partner invariably puts a damper on the Moon's feelings whilst the Saturn partner may feel the lunar individual is over-emotional. With the trine and sextile inter-aspects, the Saturn partner stabilizes the lunar individual's emotions and gives him (or her) a sense of security. Yet again, Moon and Saturn do not make the best of planetary companions and there is always the possibility of emotional hurt and rejection with these contacts.

Venus/Saturn contacts have a poor reputation in synastry, as indeed they do in the natal chart. Again this combination is often found in the synastry between married couples. In matters of affection (symbolized by Venus) Saturn can present a cold front. There is a tendency (particularly with the conjunction, square, opposition and quincunx) for the Saturn partner ultimately to reject the Venus individual. The inharmonious aspects between Venus and Saturn seem to make it exceptionally difficult for the two individuals to find happiness. This may stem from external factors, such as a shortage of money, or difficulties with family or career, which in turn take their toll on the relationship. Couples with Venus/Saturn inter-aspects tend to stay together even when any feeling or physical relationship has died. Sometimes a contact between Venus and Saturn indicates that the two individuals associate love with some form of suffering and pain and feel bound together for these very same reasons. This is particularly true if either or both partners have Venus/Saturn aspects in their natal charts. The trine and sextile inter-aspects between Venus and Saturn are easier to handle and can indicate a strong sense of shared commitment. In this case the Saturn individual stabilizes the Venus partner and provides a source of security. However, it is always worth bearing in mind that Venus and Saturn have great difficulty in merging harmoniously — thus any inter-aspect is potentially difficult.

Mars/Saturn contacts can be the most difficult of all the Saturn inter-aspects to handle — particularly if the female's Saturn is conjunct, square, quincunx or opposition the male's Mars. Saturn in this case constricts the actions and desires of Mars which makes these two planets exceedingly odd bed-fellows. Yet relationships with Mars/Saturn inter-aspects frequently involve much initial sexual attraction with an equally strong alienation later. 'Saturn can personify passion more grandly and theatrically than the most inflamed Mars', states Liz Greene, and this would certainly seem to be true judging by the number of initially passionate relationships with contacts between Mars and Saturn (particularly the more stressful ones). The ability of the Saturn individual to 'castrate' the Mars partner often lurks unconsciously in the background of many relationships with these contacts. This in turn illustrates the defensive action of Saturn referred to earlier on in this section. Mars/Saturn contacts *can* work constructively in a relationship, providing there is an awareness of the 'psychological' battle involved in this coupling. With the harmonious trine and sextile aspects between these two planets, the Saturn individual can be very constructive towards the Mars partner's actions and endeavours, but as a general rule, care is always necessary when these two planets are linked with each other.

The communication between two individuals can become difficult with the conjunction, square, quincunx and opposition inter-aspect between Mercury and Saturn. The tendency for Saturn to be over-critical can crush the mental processes of Mercury and over a long period constant carping and criticism can then seriously undermine a relationship. As a rule one difficult Mercury/Saturn inter-aspect is not going to unhinge a relationship, but if there are many Saturn inter-aspects, another between Mercury may be one too many to bear. The trine and sextile (and sometimes the conjunction) can show that the Saturn partner gives constructive criticism and advice to the Mercury individual; Mercury in turn can help the Saturn partner to understand his fears.

Jupiter and Saturn are two entirely opposite ideas, and one has a tendency to counteract the action of the other, leading inevitably to some kind of stalemate. Broadly speaking, the Jupiter partner can prevent the Saturn individual from being too narrow-minded in certain areas of his life, and likewise the Saturn partner can curtail the over-enthusiasm of the Jupiter individual. The trine and sextile indicate that these opposing principles blend well together and encourage the relationship to grow and prosper. The square, quincunx and opposition can create some disagreements and struggle. The conjunction has the potential for great success in the relationship, but not without some struggle.

The inter-aspects between Saturn/Saturn, Saturn/Uranus, Saturn/Neptune and Saturn/Pluto belong to a less personal sphere, and although each aspect has a bearing on a relationship, they are by no means as significant as those between the personal planets.

The inter-aspect between the two Saturns may not have the most important effect on a relationship, but it will show the areas where the two people are at their most vulnerable and have the most to learn. Thus one partner will be able (or unable) to relate to the other in regard to his particular set of problems, depending upon the degree of ease or difficulty of the aspect and the harmony of the signs involved.

When one partner's Uranus is in trine or sextile to another's Saturn, the Uranian partner may jolt the Saturn individual out of any rigid views he (or she) holds. The two factors combine to bring structure out of inspiration. In square, opposition and quincunx, the Uranian partner may cause upheaval and change that is resisted by the Saturn individual, whilst the Uranian individual will feel restricted by the Saturn partner, all of which contributes to some friction in the relationship.

Saturn and Neptune have little in common. In synastry the

Neptune partner tends to be an elusive and unreliable influence on the structure Saturn tries to create in the relationship. Reality and escapism are the principles involved here, so that one partner is always pulling in the opposite direction from the other. With the sextile and trine, the Saturn partner can give substance to the ideals of Neptune, whilst the Neptunian individual can inspire the Saturn partner. In conjunction, square, opposition and quincunx, the deceptive qualities of Neptune may make the Saturn individual even more rigid and limiting.

All these latter combinations give a general background colour to relationships. With Saturn/Pluto contacts in particular, unless the influence is carried out into the world, few personal implications can be drawn from such contacts. If there is a large age gap between the partners and there is a close aspect formed between the two (particularly the conjunction) the contact is more significant in the relationship. In this case there is a tendency for the Saturn individual to fear the power of the Pluto partner. If the conjunction, square, quincunx and opposition occurs between these two planets, some general resentment can develop in the relationship. With the easier trine and sextile inter-aspects, this combination can produce much mutual growth.

Hitler and Eva have seven strong Saturn contacts between them. Eva's Saturn conjoins Hitler's Venus and Mars, and squares his Saturn and sextiles his North Node. Hitler's Saturn is opposition Eva's Sun, conjunct her M.C. and trine her Jupiter. No doubt the Saturn and Venus/Mars inter-aspect was instrumental in their attraction for each other, but through a convoluted process of fear and defence, this attraction was ultimately transformed into emotional and physical hostility. Both have a strong Saturn flavour to their natal charts in regard to relationships. Hitler's Venus/Mars conjunction in the seventh house forms a close square to his natal tenth house Saturn. The Mars/Saturn square is synonymous with cruelty — a factor Hitler clearly demonstrated in his atrocities on the Jewish people. However, the outer manifestation of cruelty had its roots in a deep sense of inadequacy concerning his ability to be a forceful individual — in fact his ability to be a man. This fear of inadequacy no doubt rendered in him a sense of impotence, which in turn affected his sexual prowess. Here the astrology bears out the speculation of his homosexual tendencies; and indeed the further influence of the Venus/Saturn square supports the likelihood of his basic fear and dislike of women. Eva's Saturn conjoining his Mars/Venus conjunction and squaring his Saturn, provided an ideal peg for Hitler's complex psycho-sexual dilemma. With her

Saturn conjunct his Mars, it is entirely possible that she frustrated him to the point where he was propelled into physical violence.

Hitler's Saturn opposes Eva's Sun, forming a 'T'-square with her natal Sun/Saturn square. She also has a Venus/Saturn trine in her natal chart. Thus her radical picture describes a fundamental need for security in her relationships. With his Saturn in opposition to her Sun, Hitler, no doubt admired her Aquarian spirit, but ultimately criticized her for her unpredicatability and refusal to obey his every command. Hitler's Saturn conjunct Eva's M.C. reinforces the idea that he felt compelled to dominate her and impress his views and ideas on her. Eva, with all her Saturn contacts to his chart was equally capable of dominating him! This Saturn/M.C. inter-aspect also suggests that Hitler provided a parental influence for her — a factor reinforced by Eva's seventh house Saturn. Hitler's Saturn trining Eva's Jupiter is the one redeeming Saturn inter-aspect, which showed that the relationship could have provided a valuable source of personal growth for them both.

The strength of the Saturn influence in the synastry would have overshadowed (although not negated) all the softer Moon/Venus and Jupiter/Venus inter-aspects. These happier contacts nourished the relationship and prevented it from becoming an entirely masochistic gesture on both people's behalf. The implications of so many Saturn links indicates that Eva and Hitler shared an inescapable destiny.

The Ascendant, Descendant, M.C. and I.C.

The meaning of the four angles of the horoscope was discussed in Chapter 3. It cannot be stated too often just how important these axes are in synastry. The Ascendant, Descendant, M.C. and I.C. are the most sensitive areas in a birth chart and when these points are activated by another person's planets, this effect on the individual's being is dynamic.

In many books on synastry, interpretations are given for the planets in conjunction, trine, square, etc., to the four angles. The essential factor to remember, however, is that any planet contacting any of these four points is in effect triggering the unique relationship between the M.C./I.C. and Ascendant/Descendant axes. (This can be most clearly seen when the M.C. is exactly 90° from the Ascendant.) In a natal chart, if the M.C. is in square to the Ascendant, it is not 'in conflict' with the Ascendant — the M.C. is merely another dimension of the individual's personality structure, the role in life, the point of individuation as opposed to the persona. A planet in square aspect to the Midheaven cannot be judged *only* as a square to the Midheaven because it has a relationship with the whole psychic structure of the M.C., I.C., Ascendant and Descendant. Any contact from one person's planets to another's angles is exceedingly significant, as sensitive areas crucial to the individual's psyche become strongly highlighted.

The Ascendant is the area of the chart which provides most information about the physical appearance of the individual so that planets forming an aspect to this point (particularly the conjunction) are instrumental in the physical attraction between two individuals. The Descendant describes what we find attractive in others and has a great influence on our choice of partner and relationships in general. A planet conjunct the Descendant is by the same token in opposition to the Ascendant (as indeed a planet in trine to the Ascendant is in sextile to the Descendant). Thus the Descendant can also be viewed as a physical attraction factor. The difference in interpretation of a conjunction to either of these points is best illustrated by example. If the Moon of one partner is conjunct the Ascendant of another, the Ascendant individual will have a strong impact on the Moon partner's emotions. If the Moon of one partner is conjunct the Descendant of another, the Moon individual's moods and emotions will strongly affect Descendant individual. In fact, there is a two-way flow of energies here which succinctly illustrates the point that the Ascendant and Descendant are opposite ends of the same pole.

The Midheaven and Imum Coeli are just as instrumental in the attraction between two individuals, although neither of these points can be seen in such clearly physical terms as the Ascendant. The M.C. is the area of the chart describing the individual's idealized image of himself, which can be just as much of a powerful attraction factor between two individuals as a physical one. Planets contacting the M.C. have a great deal of influence on the individual's desire for recognition, whereas planets contacting the I.C. relate to the deepest emotional needs. As with the Ascendant and Descendant, there is a two-way flow of energies here. A person's ability to individuate (M.C.) depends upon the depth and strength of his or her foundations (I.C.). To use the illustration of the Moon's influence on the angles of the chart: if one partner's Moon is conjunct another's M.C., the Moon individual gives emotional support to the M.C. partner's personal aspirations. If the Moon is conjunct the I.C. the Moon partner instinctively relates to the I.C. partner, thereby providing support for his ideals.

Thus it should be noted that the significance of the Moon's presence on any of these four angles is that it forges a link between the feelings and instinctive response of one partner and the innermost core or essence of the other.

Conjunctions are the most powerful aspects to the four angles as this aspect involves the merging of two themes. Trines, sextiles, squares and quincunx aspects are also important of course. Contacts from the Sun, Moon, Venus, Jupiter or the ruling planet of one individual to another's angles are most propitious in synastry, although all planets in contact to these points are significant.

When one partner's Sun contacts another's angles a strong attraction is again indicated. The Moon and Venus also show much attraction and harmony — the Moon exerting a particularly loving and sensitive influence on the relationship in contact to the angles. Mercury shows that discussion and intellectual exchange are an important feature of the relationship. Mars can bring a rather forceful influence to bear on the partnership when conjunct the angles (particularly if it is the female's Mars aspecting the male's Ascendant or Descendant, M.C. or I.C.). However, strong Mars aspects are also indicative of strong physical attraction. Jupiter is a tremendously beneficial presence on any of the angles and one person's Jupiter forming a close aspect to another's angles can offset many other difficulties in the relationship. Saturn, as one may expect, exerts a narrowing and constricting influence when in aspect to another's angles, although the Saturn individual can put structure and stability into the partner's life and durability into the relationship. Uranus, Neptune and Pluto need careful consideration when inter-aspecting the angles. Uranus can awaken, but it can also disrupt; Neptune can inspire, but also deceive; Pluto can transform, but also destroy. Jupiter, Saturn, Uranus, Neptune and Pluto all provide opportunities for joint growth in close aspect to another's personal planets and this is just as true when they contact the angles. It must be remembered that people born in the same year are likely to have these slower moving planets in roughly the same position, in which case they reinforce the individual's natal situation.

In the synstry between Hitler and Eva Braun, there are several inter-aspects between the planets and the angles — some, of course, more significant than others. Hitler's Sun is conjunct Eva's Descendant, indicating attraction and compatibility. Hitler's Moon is sextile her Ascendant (and trine her Descendant), showing sympathy and emotional compatibility. Hitler's Venus/Mars conjunction is square Eva's M.C., which also indicates attraction, but as Eva's Saturn conjoins this Venus/Mars conjunction and Hitler's

Saturn is conjunct her M.C., this contact is made much more stressful and convoluted. The Uranus sextile from Hitler's chart to Eva's M.C., reinforces the idea that he exerted a kind of magnetism on her and changed her life considerably. His Pluto is quincunx her Ascendant (and conjunct her eighth house cusp), an indication perhaps that he was instrumental in her cause of death.

Eva's Uranus conjoins Hitler's I.C. and squares his Ascendant/Descendant axis, which would have been a strong attraction factor at first; ultimately, however, she became an unstable and upsetting influence in his life — a factor borne out earlier by the many stressful Uranus inter-aspects. Neptune square to his Ascendant would also have generated some confusion and instability, although initially she may have appeared somewhat elusive and highly desirable. Eva's Mercury, although square to his Ascendant, is widely conjunct his I.C. which indicates that she understood his needs and no doubt brought him round to her way of thinking when she wanted. Finally, her Pluto is in close trine to Hitler's Ascendant (and conjunct his ninth house cusp), which suggests she shared his ideals and his philosophy — although with Hitler's Saturn conjunct her M.C., it is more likely that he would have indoctrinated her with his ideals.

The Moon's Nodes

Astrologers differ as to the interpretation of the North and South Nodes in the natal chart, yet there is little doubt that the nodal axis is extremely significant. Hindu astrologers place great importance on the Moon's nodes, treating them as planets and calling them *Rahu* (North Node) and *Kethu* (South Node). This is largely because the Moon in their system of astrology takes precedence over the Sun and all other planetary bodies. Western astrologers tend to regard the North Node as favourable (somewhat Jupiterian in essence) and the South Node as unfavourable (Saturnian in principle). The North Node is considered as a 'point of contact' to be positively activated in the present life, whereas the South Node has precisely the opposite meaning. Dane Rudyhar in his book *Astrology and Personality* states that the 'North Node is the point of ingestion and assimilation, the latter [the South Node] a point of release and evacuation'.

In many ways it is difficult to understand how the North or South Nodes work in the individual chart given the aforementioned idea of 'points of contact', which is somewhat vague to say the least. The significance of the nodal axis emerges in two ways. First, when progressions or transits in the natal chart contact these points, they synchronize with important stages in the individual's life. Second, in synastry, when one person's planets contact the North and South Node (particularly by conjunction) the indications are that it is an important and purposeful relationship.

Saturn is frequently a factor in considering the working-out of karma, and the North and South Nodes may also be seen in this context. Unfortunately, karmic astrology is all too often introduced when astrologers do not have an adequate explanation. However, aspects (particularly the conjunction) to the North and South Nodes in synastry give all the indications of a fateful link. Dane Rudyhar also connects the nodes with the concept of karma. In his aforementioned book he maintains that 'The lines of the nodes show us the Directives of Destiny, the purpose of Destiny [North Node] and what is back of this purpose, in the past [South Node]'.

Harmonious Sun, Moon, Mercury, Venus and Jupiter contacts to the North Node are considered favourable, whereas Saturn, Uranus, Neptune and Pluto are inherently more difficult. All conjunctions to the South Node imply that much has to be worked out between the two individuals and that the relationship may be a testing experience for both. Complications arise when the North Node conjoins the Ascendant/Descendant and M.C./I.C. axes, as the South Node automatically conjoins the opposite point. In this case it is best to assume that the relationship is highly significant and not to be treated lightly. In my own experience any conjunction of either node to the angles implies that the relationship is a significant one.

In the synastry between Hitler and Eva Braun, there are seven contacts involving both partner's nodes. Hitler's North Node is conjunct Eva's Neptune and quincunx her Sun, while Eva's North Node is conjunct Hitler's Sun, Descendant and Mercury. In this case the fated quality in their relationship is borne out in history. Of the remaining nodal inter-aspects, Eva's Saturn sextiles Hitler's North Node and his Uranus conjuncts her South Node.

The Vertex[5]

The Vertex is the degree of the zodiac that is exactly due west of the individual at the time and place of birth. It is an exceedingly sensitive point in a natal chart. Discovered comparatively recently (by the late American astrologer Edward Johndro), the Vertex has been linked with 'fateful' or 'karmic' encounters. In my own work, conjunctions or oppositions to the Vertex appear to be the most

[5] For calculation of the Vertex, see Appendix (p. 157).

important and, indeed, the closer the aspect, the better. Conjunction and opposition aspects from one partner's Sun, Moon, Ascendant, Descendant, M.C. or I.C. to another's Vertex indicates that significant developments in the life of each person are activated through the relationship.

Hitler and Eva Braun have two conjunctions involving both partner's Vertices, but both are wide (Hitler's Pluto is conjunct Eva's Vertex and Eva's Mars is conjunct Hitler's Vertex). However, the inter-aspects involving the nodes and the strong Saturn contacts indicate a destined match in this case.

The Houses in Chart Comparison

Stephen Arroyo in his book *Relationships and Life Cycles* puts forward the idea: 'If I want to know how someone *experiences* me, I place all my planets and my Ascendant in his chart. If I want to see how my experience of another is symbolized astrologically, I place his planets in my chart.'

This is a dynamic way of seeing the main areas of life that are stimulated by one person's interaction with another. Broadly speaking, the presence of one person's planets in their partner's houses colours the types of experience delineated by the houses in question. For instance, if one partner's Sun falls in another's fifth house, the former will actively involve himself (or herself) with the creative endeavours of the fifth-house partner. In fact, the fifth house embodies the principle of self-expression in much the same way as the Sun itself, so this is a highly stimulating contact. However, if the partner's Saturn is found in another's fifth house, there will be a tendency for the Saturn partner to place limits and control on the other's self-expression. Conversely, the fifth-house partner may actually appreciate the serious and constructive approach of the Saturn individual.

Although the placing of one partner's planets and angles in the other's houses gives valuable added insight into mutually important areas of the relationship, the inter-aspects and the composite chart (which will be covered in the next chapter) are the most illuminating and informative of the synastric techniques. In fact in regard to the areas of life that are activated in relationships, the composite chart is a far superior tool for interpretation of the interchange of planets and houses and gives a unique view of the relationship itself.

Transits and Progressions in Synastry

Every time we look at a horoscope, we are looking at a frozen moment of time. In fact, the planets and angles are in continual motion from the moment of birth, which the individual reflects in his developing consciousness throughout his life. The progressions of the planets (taking one day as symbolically representative of a year) are the astrological means of pin-pointing major stages in the individual's life. Contacts made by the progressed planets and angles to those in a natal chart symbolize the time for the 'flowering' of the potential 'seed' contained in the natal chart. The progressed planets do not *cause* events, they are purely symbolic; but they indicate that certain psychological processes are due to unfold.

The flowering of the individual's potential in regard to marriage is symbolized in many ways through the progressions. Traditionally, the most typical are: progressed Sun reaching natal Venus (or vice versa); progressed Venus conjoining the Ascendant or Descendant (or vice versa); progressed Sun to natal Moon or progressions of the personal planets to the ruler of the seventh house, etc. Unfortunately, there is no astrological guarantee that marriage *will* occur every time these sort of progressions are observed in a natal chart — individuals are unique and the flowering of potential depends upon the seed. However, the progressions will indicate some important developmental stage in the life, which reflects the principles of the planets concerned. Thus the progressed Sun conjunct natal Moon may indicate marriage in one chart and divorce in another. The commonsense factors of age and marital situation are all important for the interpretation and meaning of the progressions, and of course the natal situation of the planets involved.

Transits of the planets to the horoscope also act as triggering mechanisms for natal potential, but whereas progressions are purely symbolic, in that they indicate the development of inner patterns on a particular time scale, transits have a more direct influence on the individual's life. This is because transits to the birth chart reflect the actual orbital positions of the planets at that time. Earlier in this chapter, mention was made of the Saturn Return, which is the conjunction of transiting Saturn to its natal position every twenty-nine years. Transits can be just as important (and sometimes more evident) in demonstrating that the time is ripe for an event such as marriage. For instance, transiting Jupiter conjunct the Descendant or trine Venus, perhaps even transiting Saturn conjunct Venus (if there is a natal Venus/Saturn contact). Again, common sense and the natal situation of the planets are crucial factors in assessing the likelihood of such an occurrence.

One of the strangest facets of synastry is that the progressed horoscope of one partner frequently forms links with the natal chart of the other at the time of meeting, marriage or important junctions in the relationship. One partner's progressed Mars may be conjunct or opposition another's Venus at the time of meeting, or progressed Venus in one chart may be conjunct the other's Sun. In my own case, my husband's progressed Ascendant was conjunct my Moon when we met (and married a year later) and my progressed Venus trined his Mars.

Transiting planets as meaningful inter-connections in synastry cannot be used in the same way as progressed positions, since the transiting planets will be in exactly the same position for both people. However, the transiting planets at the time of meeting and marriage do have a bearing on the relationship. The beginning of a relationship is just as much of a 'birth' as that of a baby, so that the planetary positions for that beginning can be reflected in a birth chart. This chart is then sensitive to transits and progressions. Many couples consult an astrologer in order to find the 'best' day to get married — one that will reflect their own charts and 'exert' the most beneficial influence. Even without the aid of an astrologer, couples often unconsciously choose a day and time synchronous with their charts.

There were some interesting links in the progressed charts of Hitler and Braun in and around the time of their meeting. Hitler's progressed Venus was conjunct Eva's Descendant; his progressed M.C. was trine her Saturn (in the seventh house) and his progressed Mars was conjunct her Mars/Pluto midpoint (in the eighth house). Hitler's progressed Sun was also conjunct Eva's progressed Mars. In Eva's natal chart, her progressed Moon was transiting her seventh house, whilst her progressed Venus was conjunct natal Uranus (thereby bringing out her natal Uranus trine seventh-house Mars). The fact that the progressions were more emphasized in Eva's chart suggests that the relationship had a more powerful effect on her life. At least at that time. (Hitler had no such strong indications except, of course, the contacts his progressions made to Eva's planets.)

The exact date and time of the beginning of Hitler's and Eva's relationship is unknown. However, transiting Saturn was in the early degrees of Capricorn (periodically conjunct Eva's Venus and Hitler's Moon/Jupiter conjunction) in the year concerned. This could be somewhat too generalized for serious astrological consideration, but it becomes significant in light of the fact that at the time of their marriage (which is documented) and two days prior to their suicide, Saturn was in Cancer, opposing their Capricorn planets and presumably Saturn's position at the onset of their relationship. (The progressed positions of their planets at the time of their marriage and death makes less significant cross connections.) Eva's progressed Venus trined Hitler's Uranus and her progressed Ascendant opposed his Vertex — the latter strongly connected with fateful events and encounters. Hitler's progressed Venus was a degree and a half away from Eva's radical Saturn (rather too wide for serious consideration).

Eva's progressions make strong contacts to her natal chart, however. Her progressed Mercury (ruler of her eighth house) was opposing natal Moon, squaring Pluto, whilst her progressed Mars conjoined her Part of Fortune[6] *in the eighth house. On the marriage day (shortly before midnight on 28 April, 1945) transiting Mars was at 26° Pisces (conjunct Eva's progressed Mercury), opposing natal Moon and squaring natal Pluto; transiting Uranus was conjunct her Vertex. The day before the wedding, the Full Moon had fallen on Eva's Ascendant and squared Hitler's M.C./I.C. axis. A few hours before their marriage there had been a transiting Sun/Pluto square contacting Eva's and Hitler's Ascendant/ Descendant and M.C./I.C. axes respectively. Transiting (Retrograde) Venus opposed Hitler's natal Uranus, whilst Jupiter trined his Venus/Mars conjunction.*

It is just possible that many people will consider that the inter-aspects formed between two people's progressed and natal charts is purely coincidental and little significance should be read into them. However, I feel that this aspect of synastry demonstrates the linking of destinies at a specific and 'ordered' point of time. Such a linking undoubtedly throws more fuel on the grand philosophical debate of fate versus free will.

Synthesis

Collating all the information one has gleaned from the interchanges of signs, elements and inter-aspects is a marathon and perplexing task. Inter-aspects frequently contradict and counteract one another — but then human beings themselves are full of contradictions! An

[6] One of the Arabian parts, found by adding the longitudes of the Moon and Ascendant, then, subtracting that of the Sun. Dane Rudhyar defines the Part of Fortune as 'the focal point for the expression of the power generated by the soli-lunar relationship'. Not all astrologers use the Part of Fortune, as its merits are somewhat dubious. However, it is generally considered to represent a point of happiness and fulfilment.

important theme, however, can be observed emerging in many areas of the synastry and when this happens, the astrologer knows that this is a major and dominant feature of the relationship.

With Eva Braun and Adolf Hitler, the dominant theme is Saturn. Firstly because of their mutually strong Saturns and secondly because this planet emerges frequently in key areas of the synastry. With this theme dominant, a destined and powerfully significant relationship is revealed (particularly as Saturn is involved with the Nodes), destined not merely because of their roles in history but as two people with a deep-seated bond who are committed to undergo a particular set of experiences together. Eva's Saturn contacts to Hitler's Venus and Mars (and the overall strength of the Saturn links), Hitler's Pluto on Eva's eighth-house cusp and his Neptune conjunct her Mars suggest that the sexual side of their relationship may have become the focus of their mutual problems. This, in fact, made them utterly inter-dependent on each other. Uranus, too, presents a strong theme in the relationship; Eva's Uranus makes several contacts with Hitler's chart and indeed she emerges as quite a Uranian figure hersef. Her Sun in Aquarius and Mars (in the seventh house) trine Uranus show that she sought this Uranian quality in a partner — a factor which Hitler reflected with Uranus conjunct his Ascendant. Furthermore, Hitler had an angular Mercury/Uranus opposition, whilst Eva had a conjunction between Mercury and Uranus. Their relationship no doubt mirrored the push/pull action of Saturn and Uranus with periods of emotional and physical distance (laced with accusations of sexual inadequacy). But just as one appeared to be breaking free of the relationship, the other would throw a tantrum — something Hitler was a master at, which Eva matched with two attempted suicides.

The stressful Mercury contacts probably made communication exceedingly difficult at times which must have added to the sexual problems outlined in the Venus/Mars and Saturn inter-aspects. The harmonious Venus, Moon and Jupiter inter-aspects, however, brought an underlying sympathy and understanding to the relationship, which gave them some happier moments and indeed, as I mentioned before, prevented it from becoming an entirely masochistic experience for both people. An astrologer viewing this couple as prospective marriage partners might well have felt their relationship was somewhat challenging to say the least (although, no doubt, one of immense 'growth'), but would inevitably have had to bow to the inexorable hand of Fate!

6.
THE COMPOSITE CHART

> The living mystery of life is always hidden between Two, and it is the true mystery which cannot be betrayed by words and depleted by arguments.
>
> *C. G. Jung*

The composite chart is a comparatively new synastric technique brought into focus in the early 1970s. Its actual origins, however, are uncertain. Two German astrologers explored its potential in the 1920s, but it is entirely possible that the idea was formulated and tried well before that time. Robert Hand in his comprehensive book *Planets in Composite* gives a thorough explanation of the meanings and interpretation of the composite chart. He refers to it as 'the most reliable and descriptive new astrological technique that I have ever encountered'. I support this view entirely, as do many other astrologers who have been working with this technique over the past decade.

Basically the composite chart is formed by determining the midpoints[1] between pairs of planets, angles and focal points of two horoscopes (Sun, Sun; Moon, Moon; M.C., M.C.; etc.). The resulting chart represents the shared energies of both people that constitute the essence of their relationship. Despite the rather abstract principles involved in the calculation of the composite chart, midpoints have been found to be highly sensitive areas in the natal horoscope. As Robert Hand points out in his aforementioned book (in reference to planets versus vectors), 'It [the composite] is

[1] The half-way point between two planets. In a natal chart, a midpoint can be calculated between any two planets, the result of which is a sensitive point in the horoscopic circle. Sometimes another planet is found at midpoint, in which case a three-fold idea emerges, blending together all the principles of the planets concerned. Interpretations for all the possible permutations of midpoints can be found in *The Combination of Stellar Influences* by Reinhold Ebertin, who was one of the pioneers of the technique.

based on principles that have important parallels in physics.'

Another form of composite chart has been proffered by the English astrologer Ronald Davison. This has become known to astrologers as the Relationship Chart — a meeting point in time and space between the birth-dates of the two individuals. Here no use is made of the midpoints between two people's actual planetary positions, but an imaginary birth date and time of the relationship is established, based on the half-way point between both people's dates, times and places of birth. Although some astrologers have followed his method with success, in my own experience the composite chart has afforded better and clearer results.

Calculation

The diagram below illustrates the way to calculate a composite planet.

Figure 17:

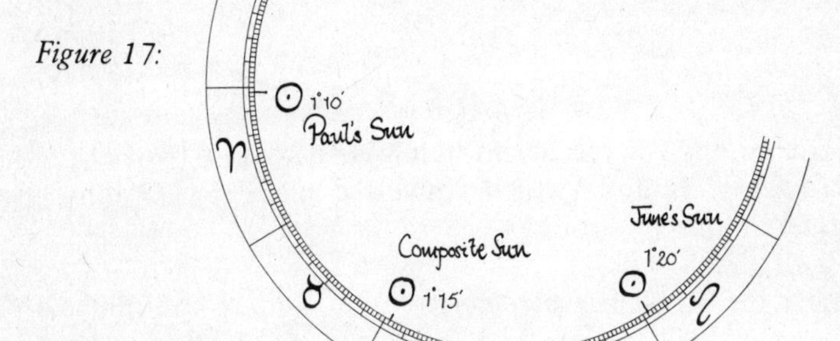

For easier calculation, both people's planets should be placed in terms of the 360° circle:

Aries	0° ♈	=	0°
Taurus	0° ♉	=	30°
Gemini	0° ♊	=	60°
Cancer	0° ♋	=	90°
Leo	0° ♌	=	120°
Virgo	0° ♍	=	150°
Libra	0° ♎	=	180°
Scorpio	0° ♏	=	210°
Sagittarius	0° ♐	=	240°
Capricorn	0° ♑	=	270°
Aquarius	0° ♒	=	300°
Pisces	0° ♓	=	330°

The position of the planet in its sign, should then be added to the 0° equivalent of that sign on the 360° table, thus giving its position in zodiacal longitude. For instance, if the Moon is found at 28° 58′ Scorpio, in order to convert this position into zodiacal longitude (or 360° notation) 28° 58′ should be added to 210° (0° Scorpio in zodiacal longitude), making a total of 238° 58′.

In order to find the position of the composite Moon, both partner's Moons should be converted to their 360° position, added together, then divided by two. The result, which is still in terms of the 360° circle, should then be converted to sign notation — the usual form in which the planets are shown.

Thus the calculation for Figure 17 would tabulate as follows:

Paul's natal Sun 1° ♈ 10′	=	1°	10′	
June's natal Sun 1° ♌ 20′	=	121°	20′	+
	2	122	30	÷
		61	15	
Therefore, the composite sun stands at (in zodiacal longitude) which, converted to sign notation is 1° ♊ 15′.		61°	15′	

One slight problem that emerges from finding the midpoint between pairs of planets is that on a circle, a pair of points will offer

Figure 18:

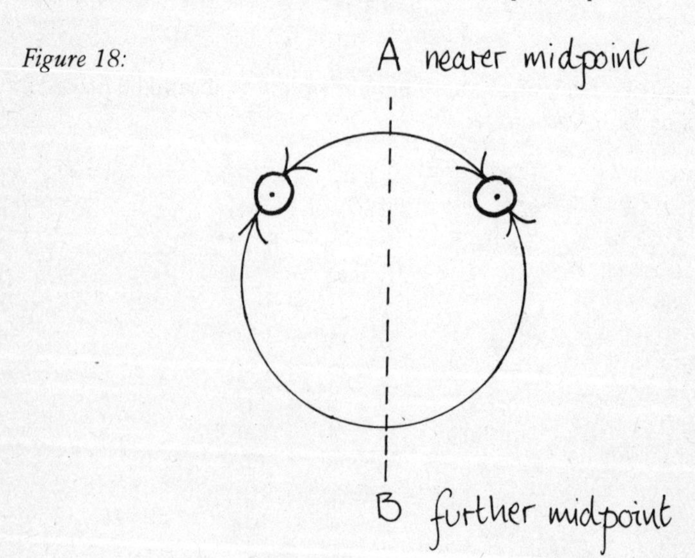

two possible midpoints. As a rule, the shorter arc and nearer midpoint (A in Figure 18) should be used. If, however, the distance between two planets is 180°, both midpoints should be taken into consideration.

The above procedure is carried out with both M.C.s, Ascendants, house cusps (if a quadrant house system is used), Nodes and the Vertex. Confusion sometimes arises with the composite Midheaven and Ascendant as people feel they can refer to a table of houses once the Midheaven is found and extract the relevant Ascendant and house cusps. This is only possible if a midpoint of both people's longitude and latitude at birth is also calculated. Although Robert Hand applies this technique in *Planets in Composite*, it is suggested here that a composite of all the angles and house cusps should be made and that there is no need to refer to a table of houses.

It is also possible to progress the composite chart by using the same calculation methods with both partner's progressed planets and angles. Thus, if A's progressed Ascendant is 15° 28′ Sagittarius (255° 28′) and B's progressed Ascendant is 21° 18′ Cancer (111° 18′), the composite progressed Ascendant will be 3° 23′ Libra (183° 28′). Although this may appear even more of an abstraction than the composite chart itself, composite progressions *do* work, as I hope to demonstrate later in this chapter. Transits, too, affect the composite chart, which will also be illustrated in the interpretations that follow.

Pointers to Interpretation

The composite chart describes the actual experience of two people within a relationship. As such, it offers an immediate and clear idea of a couple's interaction and the main areas under focus in the relationship. Certainly the other techniques of synastry already covered give valuable insight into relationships, but the composite puts it all together quickly and succinctly.

The composite can be 'read' in much the same way as a natal chart, but with one fundamental difference. In the composite chart, the planets and houses are the key factors for interpretation and *not* the signs. The planets as they are seen in composite are of course placed in the signs, but in effect they (the signs) are just abstractions serving merely to measure the planetary positions. As this technique is still relatively new, perhaps, in time, the signs will be found to have a bearing on interpretations. Personally, I have not found them to be effective.

In Figure 19, brief meanings of the houses and planets in the

Figure 19:

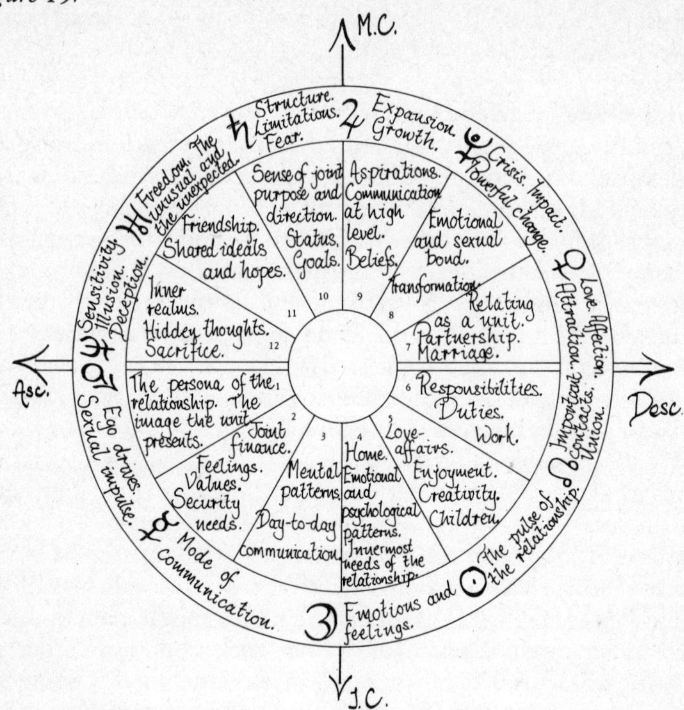

composite chart are given. The differences from natal interpretation are slight, but as the chart reflects the combined energies of two people there are subtle variations.

The angular houses (1st, 4th, 7th and 10th) are the most dynamic areas of the composite chart and in close personal relationships it is highly desirable to have any of these houses occupied. The fourth house is an especially sensitive area; home does not merely imply the four walls that surround a couple but the sense of 'being at home' with each other. As with the I.C. and the fourth house in a natal chart, in a composite, the roots of the relationship are found here with all the connotations of common origins and past lives.

The fifth and eleventh houses also bode well for personal relationships. These two houses are happy, creative areas of the composite; the eleventh house, which is synonymous with friendship, is an essential factor for long-term relationships. Although the fifth house is allied to love affairs, many long-term relationships have a strong fifth house emphasis.

The second and eighth houses have much to do with feelings — emotional and sexual — and so are also very important for relationships such as marriage.

The sixth and twelfth houses seem to cause a variety of problems for couples when they are occupied (especially by the personal planets). Duty and responsibility are factors every couple undertake in marriage, but these qualities can become over-emphasized in a relationship when there are planets placed in these houses. The sixth/twelfth axis may have karmic connotations, particularly when the Sun and Moon (or ruling planet or nodes) are present. In this case, the relationship is likely to be one of service, not only to each other, but out in the world. The twelfth house can be troublesome in composites, as planets found here tend to go unrecognized and thus frequently undermine the relationship.

Communication is all-important with two people, and the third and ninth houses are influential here. An over-emphasis in either of these houses, however, can indicate that there is too much mental discussion and not enough relating through the feelings.

The Sun, Moon, Venus and Mars are the most important planets for consideration in close, personal relationships. If there is a surfeit of difficult aspects* to these planets the relationship is unlikely to be a happy one, although it may still be significant. As with traditional synastry, the Moon is exceptionally important in relationships such as marriage. A poorly-aspected Sun may show external wrangles and problems, but they are far easier to handle than Moon difficulties (in which the feelings and instinctive behaviour are involved). The Sun, Moon, Venus and Mars in the angular houses exert an important influence on the relationship; the aspects to these planets describe whether this is beneficial or not.

As with traditional synastry, Saturn, Uranus, Neptune and Pluto need careful handling. Saturn helps in stabilizing relationships, but it can also be a restrictive influence; Uranus can be exciting and certainly out of the ordinary, but invariably shows that one partner desires the freedom the other resents; Neptune may indicate a deep, possibly even mystical level operating in the relationship, but all too frequently Neptune contacts result in deception and negativity; Pluto is a powerful transformer, but there may be mental and physical cruelty (and certainly some conflict) with difficult aspects to the personal planets.

The immediacy of the composite chart and its valuable information (which basic synastry may not fully reveal), can be illustrated by the composite of Eva Braun and Adolf Hitler (Figure 20). The chart is dominated by two 'T'-squares, one involving the Sun,

* For allowable orbs apply those used for inter-aspects — see page 88.

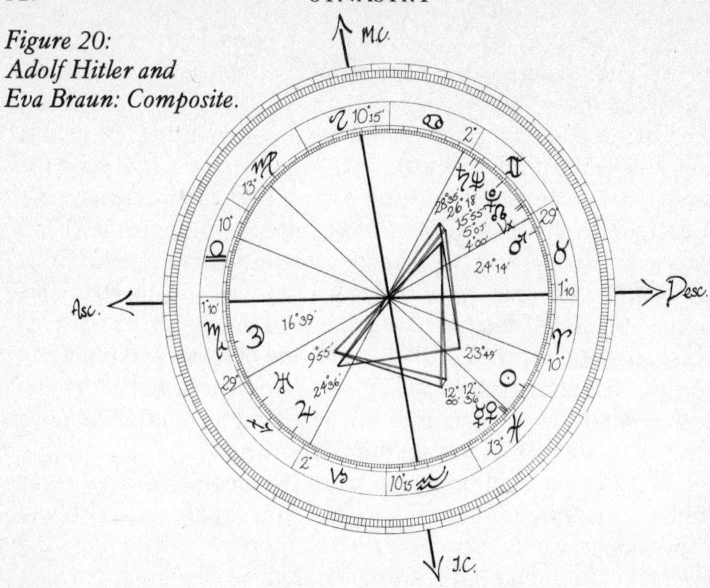

Figure 20: Adolf Hitler and Eva Braun: Composite.

Jupiter, Saturn and Neptune and the other Mercury, Venus, Uranus and Pluto. The former shows the external difficulties and peculiar circumstances surrounding their relationship (which was conducted against a background of intrigue and terror). The second 'T'-square with Mercury and Venus squaring Uranus and Pluto shows both the intensity (Pluto) and volatile quality (Uranus) of their relationship (Hitler and Eva had Mercury/Uranus oppositions and conjunctions respectively in their radical charts). As in the synastry, Saturn and Uranus emerge as strong themes — the Uranus contacts demonstrating the unconventionality of their relationship (age difference, background, etc.). The eighth and second houses are emphasized, which places a focus on the emotional/sexual side of their relationship. With Saturn, Neptune and Pluto in one (eighth) and Uranus (and Jupiter) in the other (second) — all of which are bound up in 'T'-squares with the Sun and Venus — the problems discussed in this area through the inter-aspects really come home to roost in the composite. Mars in the seventh house shows that their relationship was an ambivalent one, although there may have been a shared sense of purpose.

On the plus side, the fifth house Venus, Mercury and the Sun (the latter widely trining the Moon) indicates an enjoyment of each other and although the relationship was primarily a (love) affair, it did last sixteen years and end in marriage. (Saturn no doubt lent a hand here with a trine to the Ascendant.) The peculiar circumstances of their marriage and subsequent suicide is reflected by

Pluto, the ruler, in the eighth house in square to Venus and Mercury (co-ruler of the eighth). The Moon, too, is exceedingly well placed in the first house, showing that their relationship was an important personal one, although they may have found it difficult to be objective about each other.

Where the composite chart really 'scores' over other synastric techniques is well demonstrated in the case of Eva Braun and Adolf Hitler. In the inter-aspects, with the exception of those of Moon, Jupiter and Venus, and Moon, Neptune and Mercury, there is little to suggest the deep love and care for each other that grew during their relationship. (These few sensitive contacts had to work against the considerable strength of the Uranus and Saturn inter-aspects.) However, in the composite chart, although the difficulties emerge strongly, the harmonious energies are equally emphasized. The bond they shared may have seemed insignificant at first to onlookers, but towards the end of their lives, Hitler displayed overt love and tenderness for Eva. Eva, through no sense of personal ambition or glory, subjugated her own desires and pleasures for Hitler, ultimately choosing to die rather than be left in the world without him. That the water element was lacking in both natal charts, combined with the difficulties shown in the chart comparison, lead an astrologer initially to believe that only a fraction of their relationship was built on love and shared happiness. But the composite Sun in the fifth house (widely trining the Moon) and the composite Moon rising in trine to the Venus/Mercury conjunction, show, in fact, a high degree of sensitivity and loving care *was* exchanged in the relationship. Further points worthy of consideration are that composite Vertex and composite North Node are conjunct Hitler's natal Pluto and composite Neptune square to Eva's natal Moon (26° Virgo). Significantly, the latter was triggered at their marriage and death by all the transits and progressions at 26° of the mutable signs. Finally, the conjunction of the Vertex and the North Node in the composite chart suggests that the outcome of their relationship depended heavily on the circumstances surrounding them. That this conjunction fell in the eighth house of death (and rebirth), together with ruler Pluto, not only illustrates the aura of secrecy, violence and death that accompanied their union, but also shows that they had the opportunity to rise above those circumstances and find an element of (individual) transformation through their relationship. Implicit in this is the idea that Fate bound them together and that their love had to battle against overwhelming odds.

Figure 21:

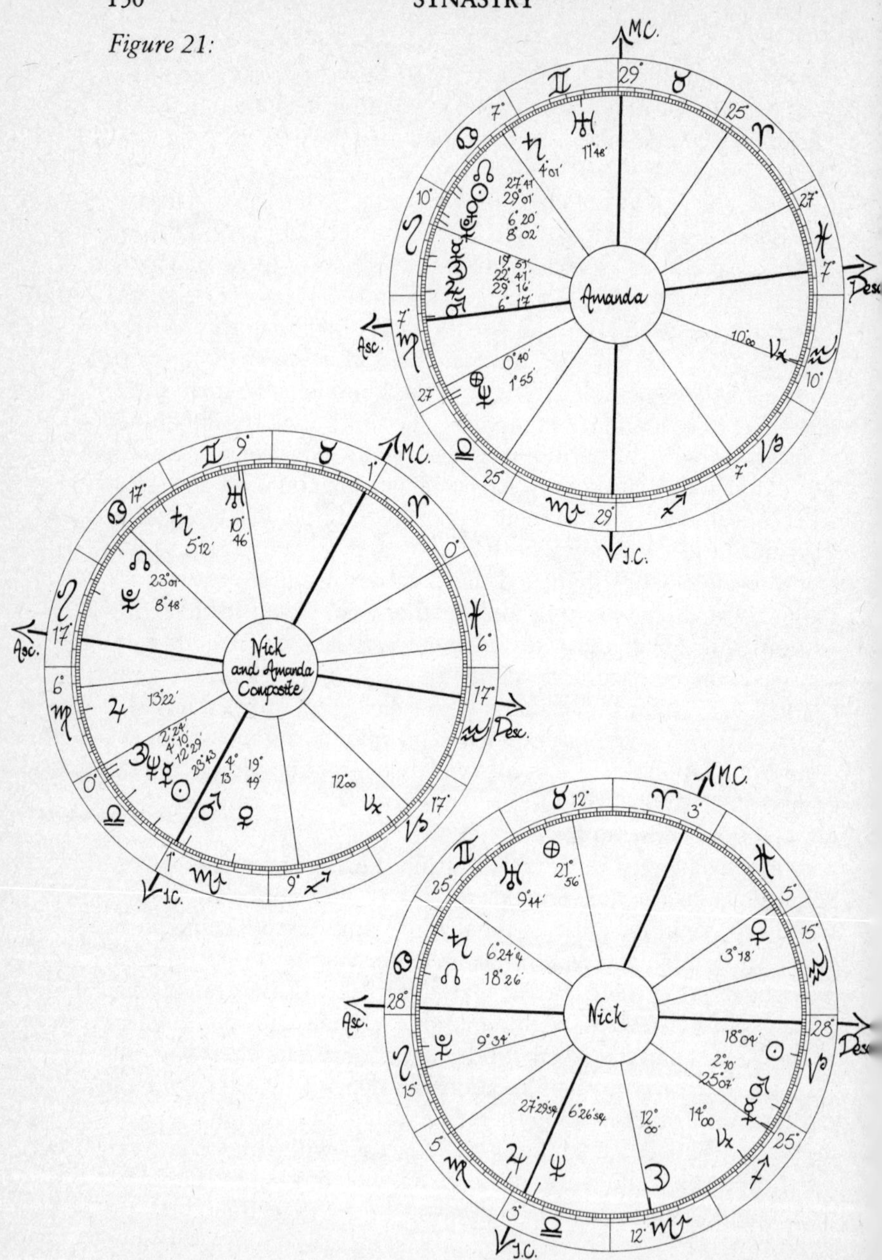

The charts in Figure 21 belong to three people who have had a major effect on each other's lives. Nick and Amanda are married and Zoe is Nick's girlfriend (Zoe and Amanda have never met). Nick is a talented (theatre) director and writer; Amanda pours her

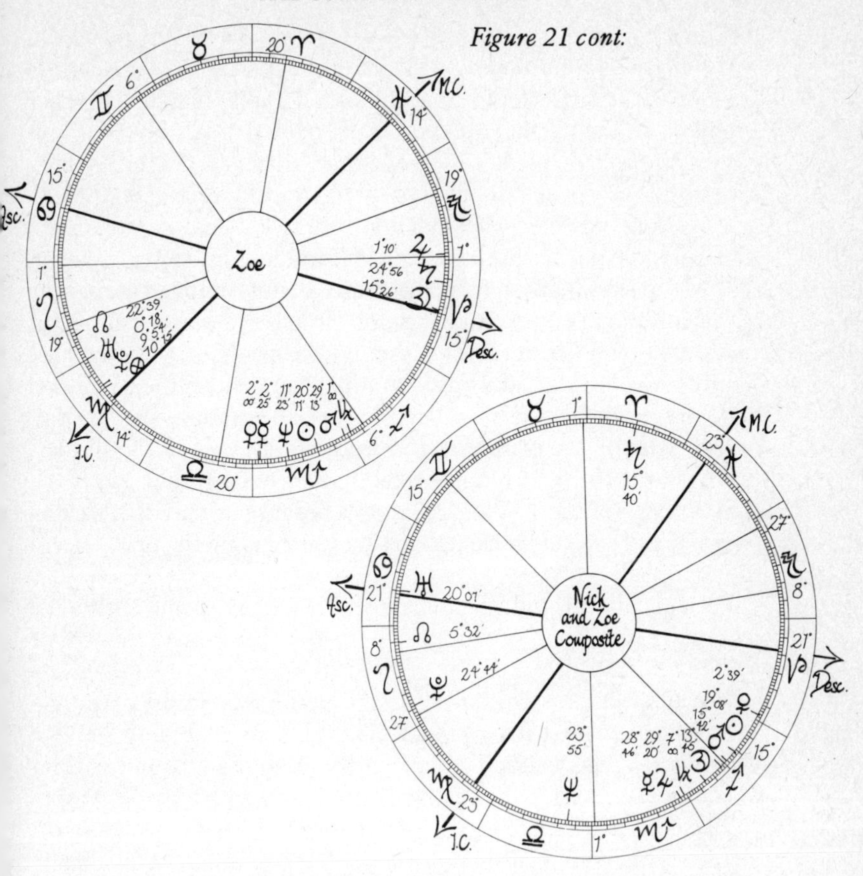

Figure 21 cont:

energy into the home and family. They have two children of their own and three more from Amanda's previous marriage. Despite the happy and successful outer appearance of their marriage, Nick and Amanda have found their relationship difficult and sexually and emotionally unfulfilling. They had been married for nine years when Nick met Zoe — a drama student who was involved in one of his productions. The relationship might well have gone the same way as Nick's other occasional 'flirtations', but instead it brought the marriage problems to a head and separation and divorce were considered.

Amanda and Nick are well-suited from an astrological point of view. Amanda's Sun and North Node in Cancer conjoin Nick's Ascendant, whilst her Mars in Virgo is trine his Mars and opposition his Venus. Nick's Moon and Venus (his feminine symbols) are not so well reflected by Amanda's chart, as she is predominantly fire, although his Venus is conjunct her Descendant.

The natal trouble areas are a Venus/Uranus square in Nick's chart and a Mars/Uranus square in Amanda's, indicating that relationships with the opposite sex are unstable and unpredictable. Further problems in the natal charts emerge with Amanda's Venus/Pluto conjunction and Nick's Mars/Saturn opposition. Both these aspects indicate problems in physical relationships, largely through suppression and defensive blocking tactics. The major difficulty in their relationship has been the lack of emotional and sexual rapport. The Moons in square signs are certainly an important factor here as far as emotional compatibility is concerned — a discordant factor reinforced by a further Moon/Venus square. As both people are highly sensitive, emotions play an important part in their physical dialogue. In the composite chart there is an emphasis in the third house, which has manifested in endless discussion about their feelings and why 'things' have gone wrong, but with no satisfactory solution. This is largely because it was the lack of *physical* and *emotional* exchange that was causing the problems in the first place.

Periodically through the marriage, Nick had become enthralled with actresses, none of whom had been a threat to the marriage until Zoe came along.

Zoe fits Nick's astrological design perfectly. She is a strongly Scorpionic female (with five planets in this sign, including Venus), which aptly reflects Nick's Scorpio Moon in the fifth house. Her Moon in Capricorn conjoins Nick's Sun and with a (wide) Moon/Saturn conjunction in her seventh house (the latter conjoining his Descendant) Nick represents the archetypal father figure, being seventeen years older than herself, and a Sun Capricorn to boot. As a further attraction feature, Nick's Sun conjoins Zoe's Descendant and his North Node, her Ascendant. Zoe's Saturn conjuncts Nick's Sun and her Moon falls on his South Node. Their Moons and Venuses are in sextile and trine respectively and Zoe's Neptune conjoins Nick's Moon — an enthralling contact, although rather unrealistic. Their relationship was a source of mutual happiness. Since Zoe worked for Nick, he was able to develop her dramatic potential and she, in turn, alternately supported and opposed his directorial views. Thus they were a constant source of stimulation to each other and their mutual involvement in the theatre provided a vital ingredient in their relationship.

The composite chart offers an excellent description of their relationship. The Sun, Venus, Mars and the Moon in the sixth house are highly applicable as the relationship was a working one and a large part of their affair was conducted in that environment. Mercury and Jupiter in the fifth house show that they took great pleasure in each other's company and in joint creative expression. At first glance, the elevated Saturn in trine to the Sun and Moon would appear to bode well for the durability of the relationship, but the close conjunction of Uranus to the Ascendant, in square to Saturn, invested the relationship with a short life — but not an insignificant one. (Also, in the synastry, Zoe's Uranus was in opposition to Nick's Venus, indicating sudden magnetic attraction, but not necessarily of the lasting variety.)

Nick's and Zoe's relationship, which lasted a little over a year, coincided with a progression of their composite M.C. to a square of their composite Ascendant and Uranus. The composite progressed Moon was in Sagittarius and contacted their sixth house Sagittarian planets through the relationship. (Zoe's progressed Ascendant was 28° Cancer, thereby forming a conjunction with Nick's natal Ascendant.) Uranus was much in evidence too, as one might expect with this planet closely conjunct their Ascendant in the composite chart. During the entire span of the relationship, Uranus transited to and fro Zoe's natal Mars at 29° Scorpio and their composite Mercury/Jupiter conjunction. Amanda's I.C. is also placed at 29° Scorpio. Nick and Amanda's composite progressed Sun was conjunct composite progressed Mars, again at 29° Scorpio. As one might anticipate, with transiting Uranus so active in all the charts, as soon as this planet had finally moved away from the sensitive 29th degree of Scorpio, Zoe and Nick's relationship disintegrated, but not without leaving its signature.

For Zoe, the relationship with Nick was her first major affair and brought out many of the potential relationship experiences outlined in her natal chart. With transiting Uranus conjunct her natal Mars, this planet not only awakened her sexuality, but provided an entirely Uranian experience with a married man, who in turn reflected her seventh house Cancer/Capricorn influence. The strong fifth and sixth house emphasis in the composite chart was thoroughly reflected in the relationship (even the ruler of the seventh house, Saturn, was placed in the tenth house of profession). The potent positioning of Uranus on the composite Ascendant implied that it was a growth relationship and one that was unsuited to conventional, long-term ties. Furthermore, the presence of Neptune in the fourth house showed that the relationship was built on ideals and illusion and had rather shaky foundations. That Zoe's Vertex is conjunct her Mars and therefore subject to the above Uranus transit, enhances the idea of a fateful experience, linked to an important and influential figure.

For Amanda, the experience of Nick's affair with Zoe was not as traumatic as she had anticipated. Although separation and divorce were considered, instead of disappearing into a hurt Cancerian shell and blaming Zoe for being the archetypal marriage wrecker, Amanda felt that she and Nick were jointly responsible for the state of their marriage. Despite her own feelings of being a passive and 'back-seat' partner in the relationship, Nick considers her a strong driving force. (With Mars rising in her natal chart, the latter view would certainly hold true.) With a Neptune-ruled seventh house, Amanda tends to place unrealistic goals on her relationships and has an over-romanticized view of marriage. Although let down and disappointed with her marriage to Nick, she felt the relationship was still worth salvaging. Through the Uranus transit to her I.C., she experienced much disruption in home life and a total upheaval as far as her emotions were concerned. However, Uranus did not completely break up the home, but instead cleared the way for a new order to operate.

For Nick, the deeply emotional and creative experience he discovered in his relationship with Zoe seemed to fill the gap lacking in his marriage. Yet some months into this relationship he was besieged with doubts and difficulties all too familiar in his marriage. Ultimately he and Amanda sought the advice of counsellors who helped them to distance themselves from their problems whilst gaining a perspective of their own contribution to them. Nick realized that his tremendous creative urge was bound up with an equally strong desire for achievement and recognition (typical of a Mars/Saturn contact in a man's chart). This drive superseded his needs in a marriage and camouflaged his inability to let go emotionally, which in turn impeded his sexual response. The excitement he craved in relationships was akin to the adrenalin boost he experienced from his career. Thus he sought this continual stimulation through new romantic encounters, which simultaneously allowed him to avoid confronting the fundamental problems. Although the marriage fulfilled his needs as a father, he did not experience the 'highs' he desired with Amanda, nor could he sustain the sensation in other relationships.

Amanda found (and still finds) marriage the one avenue for emotional and sexual exchange and was frustrated by Nick's unenthusiastic response. Once she accepted that his career drive was paramount in his life and would *always* predominate, she began to be less demanding and more understanding. Amanda also realized that she had submerged her identity in bringing up the family and lost sight of any individuality, thus she began to explore the possibilities of a career.

Nick and Amanda's composite chart is not really an ideal example of a *close* personal relationship.[2] Their composite Sun falls in the third house of communication (together with the Moon, Neptune and Mercury). That the Sun is the ruler of the chart and completely unaspected is not exactly propitious and indicates that communication between them may not be well integrated into their relationship. The need to talk over their respective day-to-day experiences — Amanda's in the 'humdrum' world of nappies and school books and Nick's in the 'glamorous' world of theatre — meant that both people met a distinct lack of understanding and response in the other. Gradually the distance widened between them and although there was a good deal of talking, there was no *real* communication.

Pluto in their composite twelfth house suggests that there is much joint suppression of energies in the relationship and although this planet forms helpful aspects to the Moon/Neptune conjunction in the third house, it also squares their composite Mars and Venus in the fourth — hence all the blocks and difficulties experienced in sexual matters. The Moon/Neptune conjunction can indicate a soul union, but with Nick and Amanda it manifested as a sort of emotional fog and made communication of their feelings to each other even more difficult. However, there is a beautiful Venus/Jupiter trine (the latter in the house of feelings and shared values) and a trine from fourth house Mars to Saturn. Both these aspects promise understanding and indicate the route to a happier marriage.

Unfortunately, the story cannot yet be completed. Nick and Amanda are still in the process of piecing their marriage together. During this crisis period, not only has Uranus been much in evidence, but Pluto has been transiting their composite Sun, thus bringing all the suppressed twelfth house energies into full consciousness. With some Saturn and Pluto transits still to be experienced during the next three years (transiting Pluto will square Nick's Ascendant/Descendant axis and Amanda's Sun simultaneously, then conjunct their composite I.C.) they will find that their marriage will be put to some severe tests. However, having emerged united through their Uranian experience, they may well grow even stronger through the Pluto transits yet to come.

[2] Incidentally, progressed composite Sun conjoined composite Venus the year they married.

7.
THE PRINCE AND PRINCESS OF WALES

And think not you can direct the course of love, for love, if it finds you worthy, directs your course.

Kahlil Gibran

This book was begun in the summer of 1981, almost to the day of the wedding of Prince Charles and Lady Diana Spencer, now the Princess of Wales. Thus it seems entirely fitting to include a study of their synastry.

The British public, goaded by the press, gossip columnists and even astrologers, had been marrying Charles off to various high-born ladies and princesses for many years. It had become something of a national pastime, rather like forecasting the winner of the Derby. After Prince Charles revealed in a magazine that thirty was a good age to marry, Fleet Street subsequently pounced on every eligible female that the Prince escorted; but thirty came and went with still no sign of a Princess of Wales. However, by the autumn of 1980, the focus of the media's attention came to rest on a demure and attractive nursery-school teacher who was spending increasing amounts of time in close Royal circles. Rumour reached its zenith in January 1981, and finally, a month later, at the end of February, Buckingham Palace announced the news of their engagement.

Until his marriage in 1981, Charles was the world's most eligible batchelor. Various romantic escapades in earlier youth had periodically come to light, giving him the reputation of being a 'bit of a lad'. His apparent reluctance to marry and the concern of his parents that he may have been following in the footsteps of his great-Uncle Edward VIII, made him the butt of many satirical (but usually good-humoured) articles and television sketches. However, one look at his birth chart (Figure 22) would have assuaged the most anguished of minds.

Prince Charles, with his Ascendant in Leo, Sun in Scorpio and Moon in Taurus (all fixed signs) takes his responsibilities exceedingly seriously but is not the type to be pushed into anything. Thus

Figure 22: Prince Charles' chart.

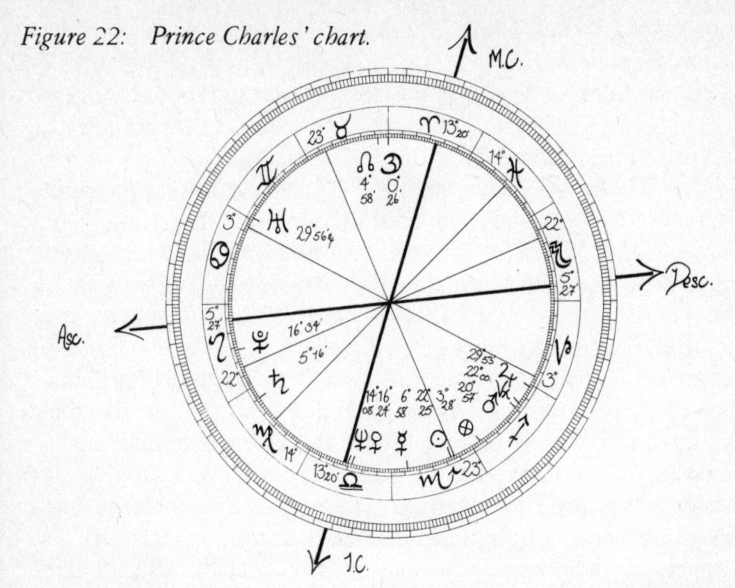

he was highly aware of his duty to his family and the urgent need to further the royal line, but equally stubborn in his refusal to marry unless he found the right person.

The 'feminine' influence is well pronounced in Charles' chart. The Moon in Taurus and Venus in Libra are in signs of their exaltation and rulership respectively and well aspected. His elevated Moon in Taurus is closely conjunct the Queen's Sun in Taurus, showing not only the close relationship he has with his mother, but the great influence she exerted on his future choice of wife. The Moon forms the apex of a Grand Trine involving Saturn and Jupiter, which bodes well for stability and durability in relationships. The Moon/Jupiter trine indicates a deep love of family and broad, generous expression of the feelings. Paradoxically, the trine from Moon to Saturn suggests that he keeps a tight control over his emotions and that he is perhaps too self-disciplined and somewhat austere. The combination of these three planets, however, produces a fine foundation for happiness and security in marriage. The Moon/Uranus sextile brings an unusual and exotic element into play, and shows that he also needs some fun and excitement in his relationships.

His angular Venus in Libra in the fourth house also reflects his love of family. Venus in sextile to Mars and Pluto and at the midpoint of these two planets, indicates a passionate nature and the need for deep and profound experiences in love. (This is also reflected by his Scorpio Sun in the fifth house, in square to first house Pluto.) Venus in conjunction to Neptune shows that he is idealistic and romantic and seeks the perfect woman. Unfortunately this combination of Venus and Neptune all too frequently breeds disappointments in love and sometimes the loss or sacrifice of a loved one. This particular side of the Venus/Neptune conjunction may have been operative in 1977, when transiting Neptune sextiled his Venus/Neptune conjunction and transiting Pluto conjoined his I.C. The previous summer there were strong rumours of a serious relationship with Davina Sheffield — herself a strongly Piscean lady (reflecting Charles' Venus/Neptune conjunction). But after an exposé in a popular newspaper of her live-in relationship with an ex-boyfriend, closely followed by a photograph of herself and Charles 'skinny-dipping' at a sheltered sea cove their liaison petered out and did not lead to the anticipated marriage.

Charles has a Uranus-ruled seventh house, yet another indication of his need for exciting, stimulating relationships with unusual women. Although this cannot be accepted as fact, prior to his marriage there had been many rumours of his alleged close friendships with married women — Uranus-ruled seventh houses frequently reflect this idea. Uranus is in opposition to ebullient, expansive Jupiter — an aspect which no doubt contributes to his goonish sense of humour and love of the practical joke. This aspect also indicates that he is attracted to a partner with an equally zany sense of humour and love of the unexpected.

During 1979, rumours again began to reverberate through Fleet Street, this time in connection with the Belgian Princess Marie-Astride. The Queen and Marie-Astride's family exchanged visits and counsel was sought of the Pope, which greatly inflamed opinion that Charles could marry the Catholic princess. (Marie-Astride is a Sun Aquarian with her Uranus in trine to Charles' Sun, neatly reflecting his Uranian seventh house; her Venus is in Pisces and she has a Moon/Pluto conjunction, the latter adding a Scorpio flavour to her nature, which matched Charles' Scorpio Sun.) In some ways this might have been a good match, but with her Scorpionic Saturn and the Sun in opposition to her Moon/Pluto conjunction (all in fixed signs) the relationship would have been rather heavy going. The marriage, of course, never came about. One can only summise that no way could be found to circumvent the 1689 Act which forbids a British monarch to marry a Roman Catholic. Perhaps this too reflected the disappointment and difficulty inherent in Charles' Venus/Neptune conjunction.

However, as 1979 was also the year that the Prince's relationship with Lady Diana blossomed, just how disappointed he was is obviously open to speculation! As a child, Lady Diana had grown up in close proximity to the Royal Family — she was born on the Sandringham Estate. Her early childhood was marred by her parents' divorce and the subsequent separation from her mother, to whom she was deeply attached. Also during her childhood, her father nearly died from a cerebral haemorrhage, the effects of which took him many years to recover from. At school she preferred dancing to mathematics and although not an academic type, she was well thought of by the staff and popular with her school mates. Her love of dancing, domesticity and children were paramount and after a short stay at a finishing school in Switzerland (cut short through homesickness), she became a teacher at a nursery school in south-west London. According to one of her school friends, Diana's childhood ambition was to marry the Prince of Wales, which demonstrates a certain prophetic ability or perhaps merely a rigid determination! Although she had been in the company of Prince Charles as a child, it was not until her teens, when they met again, that he noticed what a 'jolly and attractive girl' she was.

The Princess of Wales is a Sun Cancerian, with a predominance of planets in earth and water. In many ways she personifies the archetypal Cancerian — domesticity and children occupying the forefront of her life. Her innate sensitivity and her love of music and dancing are also typically Cancerian. However, behind this gentle and sensitive exterior lies a zany and unconventional spirit (which astrologically emerges through her Aquarian Moon and Jupiter-ruled Sagittarian-Ascendant). There is also a strong Venusian influence operating in the chart; her Sun and Mercury are placed in the seventh house and she has a Libran Midheaven with Venus, the ruler, in Taurus (another Venus-ruled sign) in the fifth house of self-expression. She exudes Venusian charm and femininity and her exciting (on occasion, daring) dress sense has become a hallmark of her personality.

Her chart (Figure 23) is not without some 'meaty' aspects, however. Saturn is strong in its own sign of Capricorn and in the first house,[1] which suggests that she is well suited to positions of responsibility and able to cope with life's difficulties (a factor apparent in childhood through the self-control and understanding she displayed towards her parents' problems). Perhaps the most

[1] As Saturn is a mere 2° away from the second house cusp, this could be seen as a second-house Saturn. Paradoxically, this placing of Saturn is found frequently in the charts of millionaires — Charles, too, has a second-house Saturn!

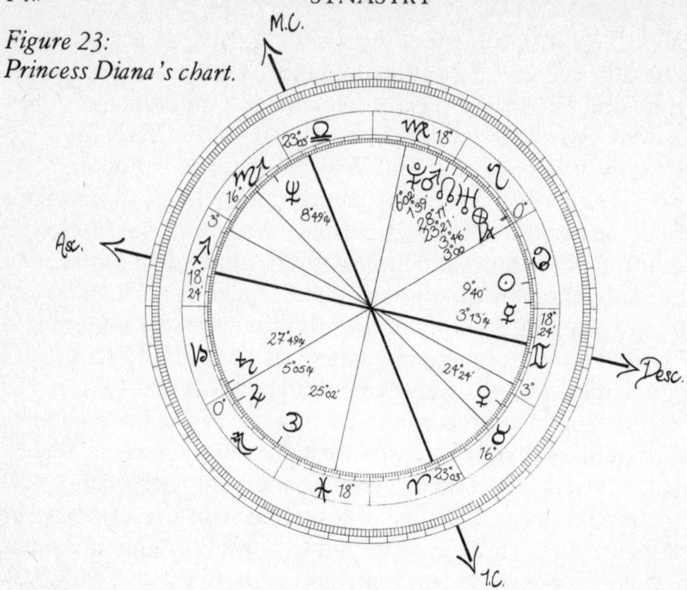

Figure 23: Princess Diana's chart.

dynamic feature of her chart, however, is a fixed 'T'-square involving the Moon opposing a Uranus/Mars conjunction, in square to Venus. Many astrologers have spoken in glowing terms about the independent, adventurous and exciting flavour indicative of this configuration (which is not disputed), but perhaps a more realistic view should also be applied. This 'T'-square, involving both feminine planets, desirous Mars and unpredictable 'revolutionary' Uranus, is not likely to permit her to slip easily into a conventional royal role. The configuration implies that she requires great freedom of self-expression, and despite her desire for security she needs plenty of stimulation in the way of exciting and novel experiences. On the one hand she may bring a breath of fresh air into her relationships through the sheer force of her personality, thus never letting them stagnate or fall into dull routine. On the other hand, if her marriage becomes too restrictive, she will break out and seek new and more exciting horizons. As a future Queen of England, the latter possibility is unthinkable yet alone practicable — but then twenty years ago, divorce for any member of the Royal Family was undreamed off!

The only relieving planets to this 'T'-square are a wide trine from the Moon to Mercury and another from Venus to Saturn. The latter aspect, although traditionally a favourable indicator of fertility (especially as Venus is placed in the fifth house), still retains some of the more difficult and inhibiting action of Venus/Saturn contacts. Thus the 'T'-square presents a considerable personal challenge for Princess Diana. She will have to find a way to resolve the dilemma betwen the urge for the new and exciting and the demand for responsibility as a key figure in the monarchy.

Princess Diana has a Gemini-ruled Descendant with Mercury (its ruler) and the Sun placed in the seventh house. The Sun and Mercury are well aspected, which augurs well for marriage. The seventh-house Sun indicates an attraction for strong, powerful personalities — a factor which Charles personifies, with his fifth house Sun and Leo rising. Mercury forms a trine aspect to Neptune and a sextile to her Mars/Pluto conjunction — the latter aspect accurately describing a Plutonic male, one with Scorpio or Pluto strongly featured in his chart. Mars is not only conjunct Pluto, but Uranus as well, in fact Mars is the midpoint of Pluto and Uranus. The combination of these three bodies presents a powerful, possibly violent theme and suggests the likelihood of exposure to dangerous situations. It is highly unlikely that Diana would generate any violence herself, so this may be a reflection of Prince Charles' chart. Charles has a Sun/Pluto square, Mars trine Pluto, and a Mars/ Jupiter conjunction (in the fifth house) opposing Uranus — all of which point to a love of adventure and danger.

In 1979, when Diana was nineteen and Charles thirty-one, their relationship developed from friendship into love. That their romance was conducted without the attention of Fleet Street for nearly a year makes it one of the most successfully guarded royal secrets. However, as soon as the media's eye was caught by the blossoming romance in the autumn of 1980, a day and night vigil was mounted on the couple, virtually compelling Buckingham Palace to make an announcement. With the news of their engagement, Britain burst exultantly into preparation for the 'Wedding of the Century'. On 29 July, 1981, the Sun broke triumphantly through London's cloudy skies and the whole of Britain — and 600 million besides — witnessed a stunning majestic pageant — such as no other nation is capable of producing — epitomizing the hopes and dreams of a depressed Britain in a symbolic expression of renewed confidence in the future.

Now, of course, with the proverbial honeymoon over, the Prince and Princess have to meet the day-to-day demands of their relationship, just like any other couple. Astrologically, Charles and Diana have some splendid links. Both Suns are in water signs and there is an even balance of the elements and qualities between them. Charles reflects Diana's chart (with the exception, perhaps of her seventh house Mercury) and Diana's exceedingly Aquarian/ Uranian emphasis reflects Charles' Uranus-ruled seventh house.

Princess Diana has an elevated Neptune, in trine to her Sun/Mercury conjunction, showing her to be sensitive, dreamy and compassionate, which links with Charles' Venus/Neptune conjunction in Libra. (This particular conjunction 'picks up' Princess Diana's Midheaven in Libra and is closely sextile her Ascendant.) Prince Charles' Mars is conjunct the Princess' Ascendant — a contact that shows strong physical attraction — and Princess Diana's Jupiter (her chart ruler) is almost exactly conjunct (within 16′) Charles' Descendant. The latter aspect bestows much happiness, success and *joie-de-vivre* on their relationship. In fact there are many Jupiter contacts in the synastry: Charles' Jupiter is sextile Diana's Moon, trine her Mars and opposition her Mercury, whilst Diana's Jupiter is square his Moon and Mercury. Thus, the relationship greatly increases their stature, both individually and as a couple.

Significantly, Prince Charles' Sun at 22° Scorpio opposes Diana's Venus (a highly romantic and sexual attraction feature); his Sun also squares her Moon and Uranus, thus providing the 'fourth leg' of her 'T'-square and forming a Grand Cross in fixed signs. Inevitably, stressful factors emerge in synastry and although this configuration indicates that there are some incredibly powerful cross-currents between them (which may result in 'block-busting' rows) the fact that Charles' Sun forms this contact indicates there is a strong and compelling attraction between them. In a sense, Charles' Sun acts as an anchor for the 'T'-square, and provides a medium through which the energy can be positively expressed. Another challenging inter-aspect between the charts is Charles' Saturn conjunct Diana's Mars and Pluto. The karmic link cannot be ruled out here, nor can the more typical Mars/Saturn/Pluto manifestation of the control and frustration of energies. Perhaps Charles' innate self-control may give the appearance of abject coldness on occasion; he may feel compelled to pull Diana into line, which may crush her expansive and freedom-loving personality. Princess Diana's Saturn also squares Charles' Moon, so each of them will have to watch the tendency to blow hot and cold and 'freeze' each other out when hurt. Both Scorpio and Cancer have a tendency to detach themselves from painful situations whilst internally brooding about them, so from time to time there will be marathon icy silences at Highgrove. Although their Suns complement each other, the Moons fall in square signs, which can amplify the emotional coldness and distance caused through the Moon/Saturn link. Fortunately, Charles' Moon is in the same sign as Diana's Venus, and their Mercuries are in trine, both of which breed understanding, good communication and a high degree of attunement to each other. In fact Charles' Venus/Neptune link with Diana's M.C. and Ascendant, and the combined Taurean Moon/Venus influence, show a shared love of the arts (particularly music and dance) and a deep appreciation of the countryside.

Princess Diana's Ascendant forms a Grand Trine with Charles' Pluto and Midheaven, which indicates that she will play an important part in his life's work and destiny. Furthermore, her North Node at 29° Leo (conjunct the royal star Regulus) is in trine to Charles' Jupiter, thus linking with his powerful Uranus/Jupiter opposition. This latter contact and the Mars/Pluto/Saturn cross link have possible implications in the radical changes both will no doubt experience in their royal roles.

Overall, the synastry shows many significant contacts — mostly harmonious. The difficulties that do emerge do not all lie in the synastry. Perhaps one of the major problems rests in Princess Diana's marrying at twenty. Her fixed 'T'-square implies that she needs plenty of room for experiment in her life. A Venus/Uranus square and a Moon/Uranus opposition in a woman's chart usually produce several romantic encounters in a lifetime, and an underlying pattern of emotional truculence. Had Princess Diana married later in her twenties, possibly after her Saturn Return, she would have had time to experience the potential of this 'T'-square without the added constraint of a marriage about her. That she has married early does not necessarily imply that she will be unhappy in her marriage, but that she may resent the ties and the excessive protocol that accompany her position. Of course, one cannot have one's fate and eat it, so to speak, and as Princess Diana's chart closely configures with all the charts of Great Britain (and the Queen), perhaps the early marriage serves a greater purpose and certainly allows her time to prepare for the powerful changes that will affect the monarchy in the early 1990s.

Charles and Diana's relationship is seen in yet another light with the Composite chart (see Figure 24). Here the major emphasis rests in the eleventh house, although the angular houses are featured. The demands that their royal roles will require of them mean that their marriage will have to withstand far more severe tests than those of any ordinary couple. With their composite Sun and Mercury in the eleventh house, their relationship not only grew out of friendship, but this same spirit of camaraderie, and their mutual interests and ideals greatly contribute to the success and durability of their marriage. The composite reflects their ability to work as a team, which is an important consideration as future

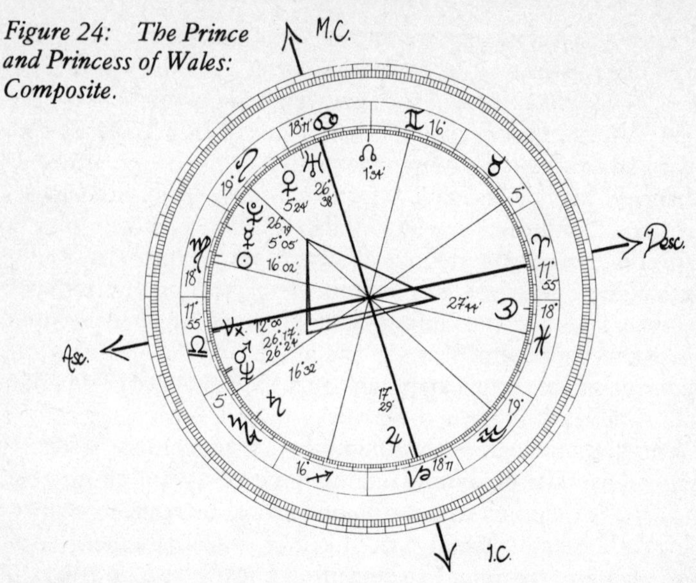

Figure 24: The Prince and Princess of Wales: Composite.

figureheads. The Sun, therefore, as the pulse of the relationship, in sextile to Saturn, and trine an angular Jupiter, engenders much stability and fortitude and shows that as a couple they will provide a firm lead for their country. Jupiter, closely conjunct the I.C., exerts a powerful and beneficial influence — the roots of this relationship are indeed in fertile soil, so the couple should prosper emotionally, materially and spiritually. In fact the position of Jupiter and its helpful aspects to the Sun and Saturn, provide a sort of indestructible support against the more difficult aspects of the composite. It is not without significance that the composite Vertex falls exactly on the composite Ascendant — an indication no doubt of a fateful linking of destinies through marriage.

Before exploring the main areas of difficulty, it is worth noting that Venus, the ruler of the chart (conjunct Charles' natal Ascendant and opposing Diana's Jupiter), is unaspected. Unaspected planets seem to have an all-or-nothing effect in interpretation and in this case Venus could support the emergent theme of the inter-aspects: that their mutually strong feelings (all too easily hurt) imbues their relationship with a love/hate quality. The other strong possibility is that since both people are artistically inclined (and as this is a tenth house Venus) their patronage of the arts will be a major feature of their relationship.

The difficulties emerge in three main areas of the chart. First there is an exact Mars/Neptune conjunction in the first house; secondly, Uranus is placed in the tenth house (widely conjunct the

Midheaven) and in square to the Mars/Neptune conjunction; thirdly, the Moon is in the sixth house and quincunx Mars, Neptune and Pluto, thus forming a 'Finger of Fate' configuration.

The Mars/Neptune conjunction has been particularly influential in the way the world has viewed them as a couple. A 'fairy-tale romance', 'a picture-book wedding' are examples of typical phrases that were on everybody's lips at the time of the wedding. They are a charismatic couple but the glamorous, high-gloss image the world has of them is of course an illusion. The danger of this illusion is that one or both people may be unable to come to terms with the everyday functioning of the relationship and therefore become disillusioned with the partner. On the positive side of Mars and Neptune, this could indicate a deep concern for humanitarian issues and much compassion and sensitivity displayed towards the world's suffering. This conjunction reflects a true missionary spirit and perhaps the existence of a high spiritual bond.

Some astrologers have voiced the opinion that sexual problems will arise in the relationship. Certainly the Mars/Neptune conjunction does little to allay these suspicions. Neptune diffuses the energy (sexual and otherwise) of Mars, which can imply that the relationship may ultimately become platonic, especially as there are no Venus/Mars inter-aspects and none in the composite. Furthermore, Saturn in the composite second house casts a rather austere shadow on their shared feelings, emotional and sexual. It is, however, exceedingly difficult to take a real stance on this issue for although the weakness of the Venus/Mars interchange and the 'strength' of the Mars/Neptune influence seem to point to a more platonic relationship, the Moon/Mars/Pluto configuration indicates exceedingly strong and intense feelings. Mars, too, as the ruler of the composite seventh house, frequently gives rise to ambivalent feelings in a relationship, and despite the dampening effect of Neptune on Mars, the sextile to Pluto and square to Uranus are powerful energy releasers.

Mars (and Neptune) in square to tenth house Uranus have important implications for the future of the partnership. Composite Uranus in the tenth house shows that the relationship will not conform to convention and that the Prince and Princess of Wales will forge an entirely new royal path. The ruler of their partnership house (Mars) in square to Uranus implies that sudden unexpected changes will be imposed upon them and that the inherent revolutionary tone of this aspect (plus the idealism of Neptune) may not only work on an inner level within their relationship, but also on their status and position in the world. This aspect, of course, reflects the Uranian nature of both their natal charts and can thus be seen in an extremely positive light. Their dislike of the rigidly conventional and staid bureaucracy will bring fresh air to the established view of the monarchy and they will emerge as two separate individuals within the relationship and not solely as a symbiotic unit. Unfortunately, the Mars/Uranus square is not the best aspect to have for a long-term relationship (particularly as Mars is the ruler of the marriage house and conjunct Neptune) — much rests on the overall strength and stabilizing quality of the Jupiter/Saturn influence.

Composite Moon in the sixth house brings an element of service into their relationship. Sometimes the composite Moon here indicates a relationship that involves much hard work relating emotionally to each other — a factor already apparent in their square Moon signs and the Moon/Saturn inter-aspect. Robert Hand in *Planets in Composite* says of a composite Moon in the sixth house, 'It suggests that [the couple] have a sense of having come together for a specific and necessary task or purpose that may not be completely pleasant . . . One person may feel like a doormat for the other; he or she is likely to get tired of that position and revolt against the other.' The latter statement is somewhat thought provoking in light of the Uranian influence in the synastry! Fortunately, the composite Moon is in trine to composite Uranus, offering much opportunity for 'growth' and many unusual and exciting experiences.

The composite Moon at the apex of the 'Finger of Fate' configuration reinforces the idea of a relationship destined to make an important contribution to the world. This configuration, as its name implies, contains the theme of fatality. The planets involved create a sort of 'energy chain', rather like an electrical circuit, which forms an underlying pattern to their relationship — in this case, possibly one of unrealistic goals and subsequent disappointments (Moon/Neptune) accompanied by high-voltage feelings (Moon/Pluto). The Mars/Pluto sextile, however, proffers the opportunity for joint transformation through the relationship, which in turn could have a similar effect on others. More than any other royal couple, the Prince and Princess of Wales will be close to the people; in fact their relationship will set a precedent for royalty of the future.

During the two-year period prior to their marriage, Prince Charles and Princess Diana had many interesting and significant transits and progressions. In 1979 Jupiter transited Leo, opposing Diana's Jupiter, conjoining Charles' Ascendant and their composite Venus. By August, Jupiter squared Charles' Sun, conjoined Diana's Uranus and opposed her Moon — Uranus conjoined Charles' Sun in the late autumn of 1979, triggering Diana's 'T'-square and activating their Uranian relationship potential. Also in 1979, Neptune transited Diana's Ascendant, imbuing her with an aura of unreality and heightened sensitivity — typical symptoms of being in love! Most important of all, transiting Pluto was applying to a conjunction of her Midheaven (which became exact in 1981). This Pluto transit represented a powerful change in direction and dramatically transformed her status. During 1980, Saturn and Jupiter both transited their composite Sun (bringing out the Jupiter, Saturn and Sun configuration in the composite chart).

By progression, Princess Diana's Sun reached an exact opposition to her natal Saturn (1979) whilst her progressed Ascendant opposed her Mercury (ruler of the Descendant). Prince Charles' progressed Venus at 24° Scorpio was just within orb of his natal Sun (although it had been exact eighteen months previously) and opposed Diana's natal Venus. His progressed Ascendant opposed her Moon and his progressed Sun trined her Uranus. Diana's progressed Mercury (seventh house ruler) was in trine to Charles' Mercury and her progressed Moon contacted his Venus/Neptune conjunction in the September of 1979. In 1981, Charles' progressed Saturn turned retrograde and his progressed M.C. formed a square to his Sun ruler Pluto. On a more optimistic note, Charles' progressed Sun formed a sextile to Diana's natal Moon and prior to the wedding his progressed Moon at 9° Cancer conjoined her Sun. Significantly, progressed composite Sun reached a conjunction of their composite Ascendant and composite Vertex in 1981, whilst progressed composite Venus (the chart ruler) reached 5° Virgo, thereby conjuncting composite Mercury and the wedding chart Venus.

The links between the Royal Wedding chart (Figure 25), the composite and the natal charts of the Prince and Princess of Wales (Figures 22, 23 and 24) are quite staggering — so good in fact, that many astrologers have speculated that the date and time were chosen astrologically. The wedding Sun at 6° Leo, conjoins Charles' Ascendant and their composite Venus and opposes Diana's Jupiter. The wedding Sun is also sextile the Jupiter/Saturn conjunction on the (wedding) Ascendant — again bringing a strong Jupiter/Saturn influence into play. The Jupiter/Saturn/Ascendant configuration at 5° Libra forms a direct link to their composite Venus ('natally' and by progression). Furthermore, as there are

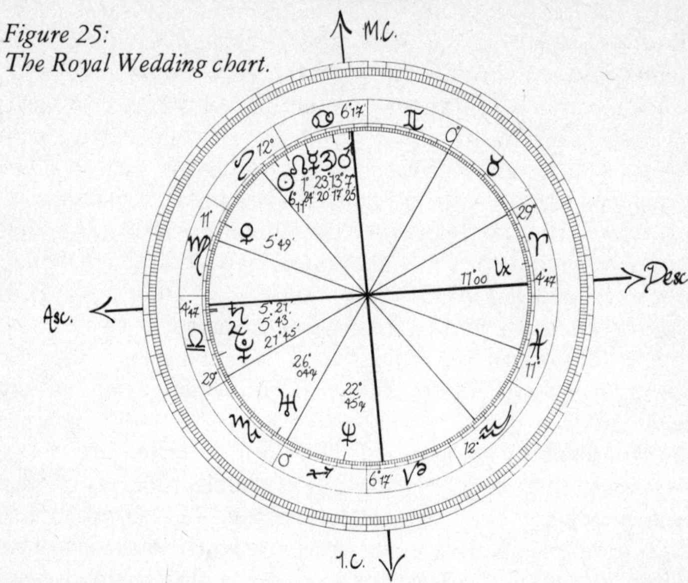

Figure 25:
The Royal Wedding chart.

various planets and points in the wedding chart at 5° of the signs, all these 'bodies' will be triggered as soon as any transit or progression reaches 5° of any sign.

The twenty-year Jupiter/Saturn cycle is known to have significance in world events and the presence of this conjunction on the wedding Ascendant not only exerts a powerful influence on the relationship, but reflects the importance of their union in the eyes of the world. The strength and fortitude that emerges in the composite is reinforced by the Jupiter/Saturn conjunction in the wedding chart, and even though Mars is in square to it, the marriage will be strong and binding. As with the composite chart, the eleventh house of friendship is emphasized, in this case because Venus, the ruler of the chart is placed in this house. In fact, Venus is at the midpoint of Sun/Jupiter/Saturn and the Ascendant, which signifies success in love. As a further bonus, the Sun stands at the midpoint of Venus and Mars — the archetypal signification of marriage and the successful (physical) union of male and female.

Though it is perhaps not strictly in keeping with a book on synastric technique, it is tempting, nevertheless, to speculate on the future. Although astrology is finding more acceptance as a psychological tool, its use as a method of forecasting cannot be ignored. The difficulty, of course, in astrological prediction is that there are so many variables that assessing the right ones can often be largely a matter of luck. Nevertheless, in studying the synastry between the Prince and Princess of Wales, I was impressed by the amount of contacts their charts (particularly Princess Diana's) made with all three of the Great Britain charts.[2] Another interesting point analysis reveals, is that all members of the Royal Family seem to have planets between 20° and 26° of the fixed signs (with a particular emphasis at 22°), as the table below shows. Thus, when a major transit or eclipse occurs around 22° of Leo, Aquarius, Taurus or Scorpio, the reverberations are felt all the way through the Royal Family. For instance, at the assassination of Lord Mountbatten in August 1979, the Moon, Mercury and Jupiter were all between 22°-25° of the fixed signs, and Uranus was near at 17° of Scorpio.

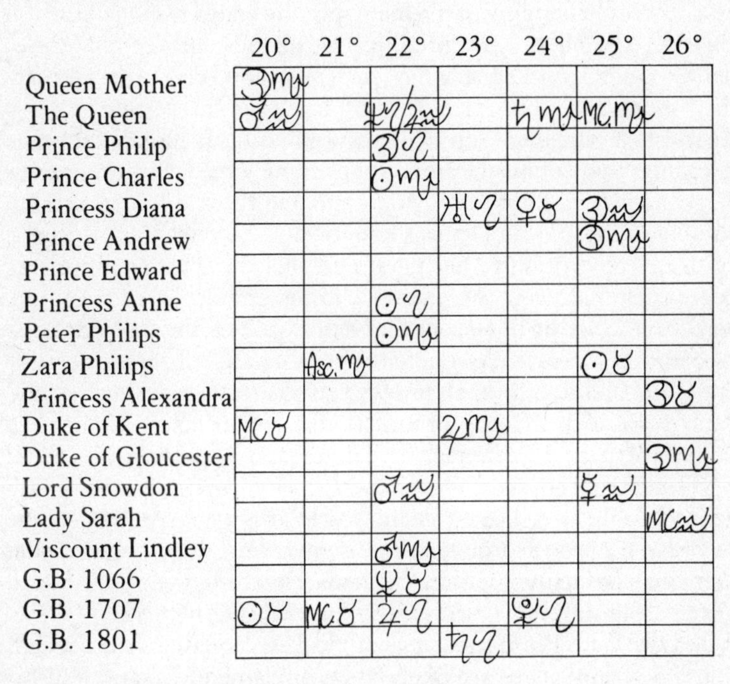

	20°	21°	22°	23°	24°	25°	26°
Queen Mother	☽♏						
The Queen	♂♒		♆♌/♃♒		♄♏	MC♏	
Prince Philip			☽♌				
Prince Charles			☉♏				
Princess Diana				♅♌	♀♉	☽♒	
Prince Andrew						☽♏	
Prince Edward							
Princess Anne			☉♌				
Peter Philips			☉♏				
Zara Philips		Asc.♏				☉♉	
Princess Alexandra							☽♉
Duke of Kent	MC♉			♃♏			
Duke of Gloucester							☽♏
Lord Snowdon			♂♒			☿♒	
Lady Sarah							MC♒
Viscount Lindley			♂♏				
G.B. 1066			♆♉				
G.B. 1707	☉♉	MC♉	♃♌		♇♌		
G.B. 1801				♄♌			

Figure 26: The significant planets between 20°-26° of the fixed signs in the charts of the Royal Family.

In 1982, Jupiter transits Scorpio, forming strong, beneficial aspects to both the Prince and Princess's charts. The arrival of their first child is an entirely Jupiterian event — Jupiter, the planet of growth, expansion and joy! In fact in mid-June, Jupiter opposes the

[2] See Appendix.

Prince's Moon and sextiles Diana's Mars, and by the 19th, Venus and the Moon both arrive at 22° Taurus. By November, Jupiter reaches 22° Scorpio, first conjoining Charles' Sun, then triggering Diana's 'T'-square. Their already great popularity will have an opportunity to reach a wider audience (perhaps through an extensive world tour) and Prince Charles will appear more buoyant, happier and self-expressive.

In 1985, transiting Saturn reaches the latter degrees of Scorpio, thus conjoining Charles' Sun and triggering Princess Diana's 'T'-square. Pluto at 5° Scorpio will be squaring Charles' Ascendant, Diana's Jupiter and their composite Venus. These aspects are challenging in the main, placing added responsibility on Charles' shoulders and curtailing the already limited amount of free expression for Diana, which may put a good deal of pressure on their marriage. The progressions are also interesting. Prince Charles' progressed Sun will conjoin radical Jupiter, thereby releasing the Jupiter/Uranus opposition, whilst his progressed Ascendant trines both the Moon and Jupiter and his progressed Mercury, the Node. Diana's progressed Ascendant is within a degree of opposition to her natal Sun. All these progressions are good ones and even the Jupiter/Uranus contact is exciting and expansive, offering new scope for Prince Charles. Furthermore, the Queen's progressed Ascendant will be at 22° Taurus, thereby opposing Charles' Sun; also, 1985 marks the year of her second Saturn Return. These progressions and transits signify an important period with many changes and opportunities, all of which centre around the Queen and Prince Charles. These changes will no doubt be reflected in the world at large (especially as the sensitive 22° of Scorpio/Taurus is involved). It is possible that there may be changes within the monarchy itself, with Charles and Diana assuming more prominent roles whilst the Queen takes a back seat. With Pluto squaring Charles' Ascendant (from a fourth house position) there are likely to be fundamental changes in his home and family, with a major move or shift in direction. It is also possible that another child could be born during this year — in which case, he (or she) is likely to be of great significance.

Throughout the later eighties there are many Uranus transits to major points on the Royal Family's charts and those of Great Britain. As Uranus is synonymous with revolutionary change, things will be altering very rapidly and suddenly over this period. By far the most troublesome time, however, emerges in the early 1990s. By 1991, and throughout 1992, Pluto will be at 22° Scorpio, conjunct Charles' Sun. This contact brings out the natal

Sun/Pluto square, which is powerful and transformative, but also violent and disruptive. During the three years 1990-1993 Jupiter and Saturn will pass through Aquarius and Leo respectively and Uranus will move between 9° and 19° of Capricorn, initially opposing Diana's Sun and the Queen's Pluto and conjunct major points in all Great Britain charts.

By 1993, Uranus and Neptune will conjoin Charles and Diana's composite I.C. and the Queen's Ascendant; simultaneously, Pluto will conjoin the Queen's Midheaven at 25° Scorpio. Also at this time (the December of 1993) transiting Saturn will be at 25° Aquarius (conjunct Diana's Moon, squaring the Queen's Saturn and Midheaven). Major progressions at this time include a conjunction of Charles' progressed Ascendant to natal Saturn and a progression of the Queen's Venus, her Sun-ruler, to opposition her Midheaven and Saturn — all of which suggest difficulties, upheaval and change. There are several possibilities open to consideration at this time: Charles will acceed to the throne through the Queen's death or abdication; Charles may already be on the throne, in which case the monarchy (and the country) will go through a period of turbulence after which a new order will emerge. Conversely these transits and progressions could work on a purely personal level and within the Royal Family itself. However, with Great Britain's charts also involved, these changes will have an outer effect on a larger (possibly world) scale.

Whatever fate ultimately has in store of course remains to be seen. The basic pattern of Prince Charles' and Princess Diana's charts contains some interesting potential. In working on their composite chart, I gained the impression that there seem to be two distinct themes portrayed. On the one hand there is a strong, stabilizing force (Sun trine Jupiter, sextile Saturn; Sun sextile and Saturn trine the Midheaven) — factors which are reinforced by the auspicious configurations in the wedding chart. On the other hand there are also some exceedingly disruptive and chaotic energies present (Uranus in the tenth, square Mars conjunct Neptune and the Finger of Fate). What this seems to suggest is that the Prince and Princess of Wales have a strong, binding relationship, but the institution they represent will experience considerable upheaval and change — some of it very sudden and unexpected.

There is a strange tendency amongst some astrologers to emphasize the more negative possibilities of challenging aspects rather than the positive ones. Thus, all the change and upheaval mirrored by the natal aspects and the transits and progressions need not be approached in fear and despondency, but with optimism and courage. All things must change — there is no growth individually or collectively, without change. Prince Charles' and Princess Diana's charts reflect the rapidly changing and uncertain times in which we live. Yet their love and devotion to each other and their family will be their greatest asset with which to face the coming changes. With their example we should move into the twenty-first century surely and confidently, perhaps with a renewed awareness of our spiritual strength and resources.

POSTSCRIPT

Synastry is a complex, fascinating way of charting the interplay and development of human relationships. In this book the basic principles of synastry have been explained, starting from the element exchange and the relationship potential of the natal chart, to the interchange of the cross-energies between a couple and the unfolding of their relationship itself. Although explanations are offered of why particular circumstances and behaviour patterns develop because of the astrological factors, the outcome of one's relationships cannot be blamed solely on astrology. It is, of course, comparatively easy to expound on astrology in retrospect, but it must be remembered that the symbols in a chart represent many levels of the individual's being — much depends on the individual himself as to how the horoscopic factors are expressed. Many times in the text the word 'reflection' has been used. This is perhaps the essence of understanding and using astrology and not being limited by it. The individual reflects the planetary themes and acts upon them according to his own impetus. In many ways the horoscope can be likened to the script for a play — no matter how good the written dialogue, a bad or lazy actor can fulfil little of the potential. Similarly, the horoscope can be seen as a karmic map with 'inherited' psychological and biological tendencies, talents and destined experiences — a structure that is permeated by each person's divine spark of individuality. This inner freedom of the human spirit allows a degree of liberty in determining one's reaction to a given situation, which in turn creates new (karmic) patterns.

That relationships ultimately serve to make us whole may sound like a modern psychological insight, but the idea has a long history in man's philosophical heritage. Plato's observation that man was originally androgynous but then divided into male and female by the gods (see Chapter 2) is a mythical version of this search for our 'other half'. Life is composed of opposite forces and everything is sustained in the fine balance between the two. Cosmic law is based on duality — heaven and earth, good and evil, male and female, etc. Love itself is the uniting of opposites — a principle one can see in traditional symbols of love, like the Chinese yin and yang and the Indian lingham. Both these symbols express duality and the reconciliation of two opposing forces. The ultimate goal of true love is to eliminate duality and separation and unite in the centre, symbolized most potently in the sexual union of man and woman — a physical expression of a deeper, more profound yearning to merge totally with another in order to experience some transcendent reality or knowledge.

The purpose, therefore, of synastry is not to dictate whether a relationship is right for us or whether it will be permanent, but to guide us to a better understanding of our relationships. In effect, every relationship is right — whether it makes us happy or not is another matter altogether. Although one may feel a natural reluctance and hesitation about entering a relationship astrologically indicated as being difficult, the difficulties are no doubt essential to both individuals' experience, and as we have seen, 'growth' is more often achieved through pain and confrontation than through ease, which requires no personal effort or struggle. It could be argued of course, that since astrology can show the inherent potential of a relationship, it must be possible, indeed advisable, to avoid entering difficult relationships. To escape one's Fate (even if one had any real choice in the matter) would no doubt lead to a deferral of the experience or to meeting a similar situation in another relationship. Thus, every relationship holds the potential for creating more understanding, self-knowledge and harmony within oneself, and synastry is a fine means of gaining a perspective on the relevant issues. However, until we, as individual mortals, have reached an enlightened state and have made contact with our Source, I suspect Fate will continue to retain the upper hand.

APPENDIX

		Quadruplicity/Quality	*Triplicity/Element*
ARIES	♈	CARDINAL	FIRE
TAURUS	♉	FIXED	EARTH
GEMINI	♊	MUTABLE	AIR
CANCER	♋	CARDINAL	WATER
LEO	♌	FIXED	FIRE
VIRGO	♍	MUTABLE	EARTH
LIBRA	♎	CARDINAL	AIR
SCORPIO	♏	FIXED	WATER
SAGITTARIUS	♐	MUTABLE	FIRE
CAPRICORN	♑	CARDINAL	EARTH
AQUARIUS	♒	FIXED	AIR
PISCES	♓	MUTABLE	WATER

SUN	☉	rules ♌	exalted ♈	detriment ♒	fall ♎
MOON	☽	rules ♋	exalted ♉	detriment ♑	fall ♏
MERCURY	☿	rules ♊ ♍	exalted ♍	detriment ♐	fall ♓
VENUS	♀	rules ♉ ♎	exalted ♓	detriment ♈	fall ♍
MARS	♂	rules ♈	exalted ♑	detriment ♎	fall ♋
JUPITER	♃	rules ♐	exalted ♋	detriment ♊	fall ♑
SATURN	♄	rules ♑	exalted ♎	detriment ♋	fall ♈
URANUS	♅	rules ♒	exalted ♏	detriment ♌	fall ♈
NEPTUNE	♆	rules ♓	exalted ♌	detriment ♍	fall ♒
PLUTO	♇	rules ♏	exalted —	detriment ○	fall —

NORTH NODE	☊
VERTEX	∨
PART OF FORTUNE	⊕
ASCENDANT	Asc.
DESCENDANT	Desc.
MIDHEAVEN	M.C.
IMUM COELI	I.C.

Chapter 1

Houses
The 360° circle of the horoscope is divided into twelve sections — houses. The rising degree (Ascendant) marks the beginning (cusp) of the first house, the remaining eleven houses follow on from this point. The first house correlates in basic meaning to the sign Aries, the second Taurus, the third, Gemini, and so on. Astronomically, the houses represent the twelve divisions of the diurnal (daily) circle against the Ecliptic.

Chapter 2

Vivien Leigh: 5 November, 1913, Darjeeling, India, 5.16 p.m. local time. 88E29 26N58.
Source: Profiles of Women, Lois Rodden.

Lord Olivier: 22 May, 1907, Dorking, England, 5.00 a.m. GMT. OW20 51N14.
Source: American Book of Charts, Lois Rodden.

Adolf Hitler: 20 April, 1889, Brannau, Austria, 6.30 p.m. local time. 13E03 48N16.
Source: Birth Certificate.

Eva Braun: 6 February, 1912, Munich, Germany, 12.30 a.m. local time. 11E33 48N09.
Source: Birth Certificate, Profiles of Women, Lois Rodden. There is also a birth date of 7 February, 1912, 2.25 a.m. quoted for Eva. This is taken from a Doctor's memoirs (perhaps somewhat unreliable) and appears in *Eva and Adolf* by Glenn Infield. This latter chart produces less significant results as far as the synastry with Hitler is concerned or the progressions and transits.

Chapter 4

Princess Margaret: 21 August, 1930, Glamis, Scotland, 9.22 p.m. BST. 3W01 56N37.
Source: Buckingham Palace.

Chapter 5

Clark Gable: 1 February, 1901, Cadiz, Ohio, 5.30 a.m. CST. 81W00 40N16.
Source: The American Book of Charts, Lois Rodden.

Carole Lombard: 6 October, 1908, Fort Wayne, Indiana, 3.30 a.m. CST. 85W09 41N04.
Source: Profiles of Women, Lois Rodden.

Humphrey Bogart: 23 January, 1899, New York, N.Y., 1.40 p.m. EST. 73W57 40N45.
Source: The American Book of Charts, Lois Rodden.

Lauren Bacall: 16 September, 1924, New York, N.Y., 3.00 a.m. EDT. 73W57 40N45.
Source: Profiles of Women, Lois Rodden.

Vertex Calculation. — Subtract the birth latitude from 90° (which gives the co-latitude). Using a Table of Houses for the new latitude, find the M.C. that corresponds to the I.C. in the birth chart and extract the relevant Ascendant for that M.C. The resultant Ascendant is the Vertex.

Chapter 6

Prince Charles: 14 November, 1948, London, 9.14 p.m. GMT. 51N 0W08 51N32.
Source: Buckingham Palace.

Princess Diana: 1 July, 1961, Sandringham, England, 7.45 p.m. BST. OE30 52N50.
Source: Buckingham Palace. A time of 2.00 p.m. was first given for the Princess of Wales, but subsequently found to be in error.

The Prince and Princess of Wales' Wedding chart: 29 July, 1981, London, 11.00 a.m. BST 0W08 51N32.

There are three main charts in use for Great Britain:

1. *The Coronation of William I:*
   25 December 1066, noon Westminster.
   ☉9° ♑55′; ☽29° ♓08′; ☿ 16° ♑39′; ♀ 29° ♑53′; ♂8° ♒28′; ♃ 7° ♍57′♃; ♄ 16° ♍50′♃; ♅ 28° ♐ 27′; ♆22° ♉12′♃; ♇3° ♓52′; ☊19° ♍16′♃; M.C. 8° ♑42′; Asc. 22° ♈.17′.

2. *The Union of England and Scotland.*
   1 May, 1707, 0 hrs. 0 mins. London.
   ☉20° ♉29′; ☽28° ♍10′; ☿ 11° ♉04′♃; ♀ 6° ♈49′; ♂20° ♋01′; ♃ 21° ♌51′; ♄ 5° ♊06′; ♅ 9° ♌24′; ♆22° ♈06′; ♇ 23° ♌00′; M.C. 21° ♏; Asc. 16° ♑.

3. *The Act for the Union of Great Britain and Ireland.*
   1 January, 1801, Greenwich. 0 hrs. 0 mins. Greenwich.
   ☉10° ♑11′; ☽ 19° ♋29′; ☿ 17° ♐36′; ♀ 16° ♒32′; ♂11° ♉47′; ♃ 1° ♌58′♃; ♄ 23° ♌17′♃; ♅ 2° ♎16′♃; ♆18° ♏43′; ♇ 5° ♓00′; M.C. 9° ♋′; Asc. 7° ♎10′.

RECOMMENDED READING LIST

For Beginners

Sheila Geddes. *The Art of Astrology*, Aquarian Press (1980).

Alan Oken. *The Horoscope, The Road and its Travellers*, Bantam (1974).

Derek and Julia Parker. *The Compleat Astrologer*, Mitchell Beazley (1971).

Frances Sakoian and Louis Acker. *The Astrologer's Handbook*, Peter Davies (1973).

General

Stephen Arroyo. *Astrology, Psychology and the Four Elements*, CRCS Publications (1975).

Stephen Arroyo. *Astrology, Karma and Transformation*, CRCS Publications (1978).

Liz Greene. *Saturn*, Samuel Weiser (1976).

Robert Hand. *Horoscope Symbols*, Para Research (1981).

Synastry

Liz Greene. *Relating*, Coventure (1977).

Robert Hand. *Planets in Composite*, Para Research (1975).

Lois Haines Sargent. *How to Handle Your Human Relations*, A.F.A. (1958).

Reference and Research

Geoffrey Dean. *Recent Advances in Natal Astrology*, The Astrological Association (1977).

INDEX